Janis' writing PULLS YOU INTO THE BEAUTY OF GOD in great depth! She continually encourages to get the focus off of self towards God and His Kingdom. Her writing is LAYERED WITH INVITATION again and again as she comes at it from different angles.

God is definitely extending an invitation, in a GENTLE AND LOVELY way, to all who are reading, to come into His arms of love, safety, and truth.

Possibilities to comprehend that He is real for each are found within *Learning to Be Loved*, not just addressing the mind, but the spirit, as well as the heart, INVITING INTO THE REALM OF GOD'S KINGDOM.

—Theora Meyers,
House of Intrepid, Calgary (currently)
Canadian Prophetic Council,
Extreme Prophetic, RedLeaf Prayer,
One Heart Ministerial of Calgary (formerly)

In *Learning to Be Loved*, Janis Gilbertson bravely tells us her story of coming to a place of profound healing. She shares her stories with HONESTY, GRACE, HUMOUR AND VULNERA-BILITY. She also shares with us and expounds on specially chosen experiences, verses and quotes that have had a deep impact on her. And she explains how her spirituality and relationship with Jesus (and her cat!) has given her a safe haven to weather her emotional storms. Her writing holds acceptance of self and provides ENCOURAGEMENT TO OTHERS on their own healing journey.

Janis has a FIERCE HEART and is a SURVIVOR. This shines through in her writing, encouraging all of us to meet our journey where we are at and to TAKE A CHANCE at beginning the baby steps that will help us to emerge from our protective shell and begin to heal at our own pace.

—Onalea Gilbertson,
Creator, Performer, Director

HONEST, OPEN, VULNERABLE, drawing into Holy Spirit, intellectual, sincere, autobiographical, CREATIVE AND INSPIRING!

—Patricia Hrynkiw,
Senior Instructor of Voice at the University of Calgary,
Author, *How My Dog Taught Me to Sing*

Learning to Be Loved is BEAUTIFUL.... If no one knew Janis intimately before reading *Learning to Be Loved*, they surely will at the end. Her love for words AMAZES ME!!! So POETIC, DESCRIPTIVE, so FULL OF LOVE, truth, realness. Her love for scripture, for INTIMACY WITH THE FATHER, BRINGS A LONGING to us as readers to experience the same. I love Janis' description of Pip and the parallels between both their journeys. I love her challenges and questions for the reader. I love her sharing her journaling and the rawness, the beauty and the poetry. I know many will be blessed as you journey with Janis from a PEA floating in a Pod, to the beauty of PIP and to the PRINCESS that has evolved.

—Daphne Clark,
former Senior Leader CTF, Calgary,
Blue Diamond Leader Doterra Essential Oils

What a WONDERFUL TESTIMONY! In this book, Janis shares her experience of healing as she encounters the voice of the Wonderful Counselor. This book containing her story demonstrates that Jesus is alive today and is truly the healer of our hearts, the restorer of our souls and the deliverer of our lives. Jesus has given Janis a new life, and this is her testimony of the words He has spoken and the life He has given. May each reader also ENCOUNTER THE HEALING WORDS OF THE WONDERFUL COUNSELOR.

—Dr. Mark Virkler,
Communion with God Ministries

I've always been surprised and blessed by the courage Janis and her husband Grant have displayed in the time that we have known them. While wading through a lifetime of challenges, they remained present with Holy Spirit and have allowed Him to speak, and then they actually believed what He said and trusted Him and His process.

It's not really about us getting it right; it's about allowing our Dad the time and space to get it right in and for us, and this was captured so well in this book. The inclusion of personal journaling makes it DOWN TO EARTH, REAL, HOPEFUL. Hopeful, that I as the reader can, too, begin to hope again. Real, because it is possible to drop the defences, let the walls down, and be led as a child by Holy Spirit. Down to earth, because THIS IS FOR EVERYONE regardless of social or spiritual status.

The JOURNEY OF THE HEART is one in which our Father sees and heals us inside when man only sees the outside, and *Learning to Be Loved* displays so beautifully this deep, inward journey. This book will be the inspiration and permission that many need to immerse themselves in the Father's presence and journey He has for them.

—Darrin Clark,
former Senior Leader CTF Calgary,
President, Mercy Mandate Foundation

[Janis is] a VERY GIFTED WRITER, and writing largely in [poetic] prose is quite the feat.

—Steve Long,
Senior Leader CTF Toronto

Are you YEARNING to be Loved? Do you know how much the FATHER LOVES YOU and DESIRES for YOU to KNOW HIM? If this is your heart's cry then PICK UP this book!

Janis shares her story of being DRAWN INTO this ALL-CONSUMING LOVE. Her painful journey of discovery entices to EXPLORE the DEPTH of His love and to abandon all in simple, child-like TRUST. Delve deeper into this personal pilgrimage with her as YOU TOO come to the realization of BEING LOVED, living loved.

It is best summed up in these words from *Learning to BE LOVED*:

"Come up here. Come away with Me My fair one, My beloved. Come and sit with Me. Come and rest with Me, lean back into Me. Let yourself be carried - as a pea in a pod in the stream of Life - My very Living Waters, the place you are designed to be. I will rest you, restore you, I will bring you to Life, alive and seeing from My wider viewpoint. You shall know My peace."

—Zelda Duursema
author of *Death, Where is Your Victory?*

Finding Your Way From Distressed To Rest

learning
to *BE*
LOVED

Janis Pocock Gilbertson

ISBN softcover: 978-1-953314-83-3

ISBN ebook: 978-1-953314-35-2

Library of Congress Control Number: 2020922387

Published by:

Messenger Books
30 N. Gould Ste. R
Sheridan, WY 82801

CONTENTS

ACKNOWLEDGMENTS

Thank you!!

Unlocking Your Book/Messenger Books Publishing! Jeremiah and Teresa Yancy, Krissy Nelson, Liz, Rebecca, ALL your team – There just aren't enough words to express the gift that you have brought to fledgling writers, to me. Your continual gracious honouring, encouraging, teaching, mentoring, making opportunity for unexpected exponential growth, that each one could develop the message gift God had given within to express in their own unique voice. Stunning. Thank you Wendy Duncan for your editorial guidance through the refining of *Learning to Be Loved*. I'm so pleased and thankful that God put you on my team!

Patricia Hrynkiw –Thank you for your responsive to Holy Spirit timely prompt to me for writing my 'inspirational book', and for all your creative encouragements along the way. Your faith-life example is Powerful. Thank you too for being a willing first editor of *Learning to Be Loved*.

Theora Meyers — With your face toward Jesus, your vulnerable seeing heart, you live and walk the culture of honour as few do. Thank you for releasing the call of Spirit: "I want you to lay your vision to heart" in January 2018. In it I heard not only permission and invitation to step into the gift and focus of writing, creating with words, but His command to do so – "THIS is who I've created you to be and the vehicle for you to speak through. Consider it as your job, your Work, your University Graduate Studies, requiring all your focus and attention – it is to take precedence over everything else – be diligent to honour this time!" and *Learning to Be Loved* began conception.

Thank you, Marie Taylor, daughter Onalea, Steve Long, and Mark Virkler, for agreeing to wade through the wordy unedited first draft of *Learning to Be Loved*. Your insights and advice encouraged and challenged me to keep going. Thank you, Zelda Duursema and Jen Franklin. Your very thoughtful feedback got me out of a quagmire of confusion!

Darrin Derksen – Thank you for using your gifts and training in helping me through the most vulnerable experience of revelation in my life, for your lack of pushing even one iota, your guiding into invitation to allow Jesus to show Himself in the deepest place of offense and impact, into seeing what He did afterwards, and then your guiding through the journey of forgiveness toward healing – I am profoundly, eternally thankful.

Kathryn Solomon — Fierce fervent friend, intercessor, caregiver and lover of Pip! You example daily the generous, giving heart of God and the sacrifice of praise-filled thanksgiving!

Thank you Darrin and Daphne Clark – God used the capsule in time that was Catch the Fire, Calgary, to get past the walls of self-protection I'd built within over many years. You allowed each one in front of you to be just who they were, where they were, ridiculously no requirements, judgments, criticisms, or rules to follow. Blew my mind! Many walls of expectation and requirements, performance (& failure) were exposed in me and I simply kept hearing more freedom to truly know, receive and live from the easy, healing love of God. I don't think *Learning to*

Be Loved would be what it is, may not even BE, if we hadn't 'done life together' for those few years.

Jan Fischer – you were the first to hear and speak to me that Holy Spirit was calling to Rest, Refreshment, Restoration – and you offered your companionship along the way. Together with your hubby John, Diane & Fred Van Vliet, and Dorothea Hopf, I thank each of you for our journey of Connecting, for listening for Father's heart together, and the encouragement to Write, Dance and Fly! There is so much of our Dad in each of you. You are very dear to me.

Thank you little grandson Salix – for the upfront right-before-our-eyes example and revelation of what it is "to be as a little child" and all that has added to understanding the incredible freedom, joy and single-minded expression of the invitation to the love that God calls each of us to. Through living life with you Salix, I recognised the ferociousness of God's heart on our behalf – NannaPoppa's love and delight in you is profound; can our Creator Father's be any less so for us?!!

All you precious, unique gifts of God friends who have loved, cried, and laughed life with me. I want to name you all but do not want to inadvertently leave a name out so I'll just say: if we've giggled, talked, prayed, played, wept, danced, listened, worshiped, walked, been silent arm in arm together these last few years of love discovery – it's you! Thank you everyone; my heart is full: I've seen our Dad's beauty and gift in every single one of you.

My Grant — I've learned and received so much of the love of God through you - mostly His playfulness (especially through your 'Why Not?' dream!). Thank you for loving me out of my frequently deadly seriousness (I still need reminders from time to time...). Thank you for being willing for pretty much anything, for never (hardly ever) saying no, for mountain loads of encouragement. You have always been gift!

Thank You Trinity – Loving Abba, Caring Papa, Faithful Father; King Jesus, Redeeming playful Friend, tender Bridegroom, Fierce Defender, all my Peace; Holiest Spirit, Teacher, Healer, Janis Whisperer, Soother of my soul, Vision to my heart.

And so much MORE.

> "Receiving a gift is like getting a rare gemstone; any way you look at it, you see beauty refracted."
>
> — PROVERBS 17:8, MSG

The beauty of God shines through each one of you; you are all gifts! Thank you from the bottom of my heart.

DEDICATION

*"As Jesus was having a meal in Matthew's house,
many tax collectors and sinners came and ate with Jesus
and his disciples. When the Pharisees saw this they said to
his disciples, "Why does your teacher eat with tax collectors
and sinners?" When Jesus heard this he said,
"Those who are healthy don't need a physician,
but those who are sick do."*
Matthew 9:10-12, NET

The note on Matthew 9:12 in the New English Translation says, "Jesus' point is that he associates with those who are sick because they have the need and will to respond to the offer of help. A person who is healthy (or thinks mistakenly that he is) will not seek treatment."[1]

Learning to Be Loved is dedicated to all those who know they are not well—the struggling, at the end-of-their-rope hurting ones and all who long desperately for relief, hoping against hope for Hope.

It is dedicated as well to my children. Onalea, Leif, Arianna, and Lucas ~ You have each been anointed creative Words written on the pages of my life. Every one of you has inspired me greatly not to remain hidden but to release what was within. Thank You! It is my prayer that you are inspired, too!

FOREWORD

In her book, Janis shares aspects of her life journey, which may differ from yours, yet you will be encouraged by scriptures, poetry, stories, and artwork that will inspire you as you are *Learning to Be Loved*, as you face trials, and as you move towards restoration and healing. Despite difficult circumstances, trauma, and fear, Janis found herself being pursued by God. He was inviting her to learn to be still, hear His voice, and find delight in His promises. Janis invites you to engage these truths with intentional pauses and reflections so that in the midst of reading, you too can experience the love of the Father, who is also pursuing and speaking to you. My hope is that you will discover the blessing of being loved along your own life journey.

—Darrin Derksen, MA, RCC
(Counselling Psychology)
Live 2B Free
Counselling Services Provider
(BCACC Registered Clinical Counsellor)
Abbotsford, BC

Arise [from the depression and prostration in which circumstances have kept you—rise to a new life]! Shine (be radiant with the glory of the Lord), for your light has come, and the glory of the Lord has risen upon you!

Isaiah 60:1, AMPC

Arise My love, My fair one, And come away to climb the rocky steps of the hillside. O My dove, here in the clefts of the rock, in the sheltered and secret place of the steep pathway, Let Me see your face, Let Me hear your voice; For your voice is sweet, And your face is lovely.

Song of Songs 2:13-14, AMP

My heart says of You, "Seek His face!" Your face, LORD, I will seek!

Psalm 27:8, NIV

INTRODUCTION

Welcome!

A few years ago, as I sat and read with the Trinity, I recognised clearly that when He spoke and called us His Beloved, there is included in that title the injunction, direction, and challenge to BE Loved. I've been captured by that, surprised to find that in some ways it is surprisingly difficult to actually receive love.

This book is similar to the maps created by cartographers of old when new lands were found. It is a charting of my journey with God over a period of almost five years. This journey encompassed much emotion—from painful depths to glorious, joy-filled heights—as Holy Spirit of Living God illuminated and revealed, touched and brought healing to old wounds long unrecognised. He led me to a deeper discovery of God our Father's huge heart through words, music, His still small voice, and more. He brought me into the revelation of what it is to truly Be Loved.

Selah

I've always loved the word Selah. This word invites me to quietness, into a stillness infused with fragrant beauty as the Presence of God fills the space opened up to Him.

- *Selah* is used 71 times in Scripture. It appears in 39 psalms, and three times in Habbakkuk 3.[1] It has been described as a musical direction; the Psalms are songs after all, and all music needs direction to bring out its best sound and delivery! It is thought that *Selah* could designate a place for an instrumental musical interlude: a pause before moving on to the next movement or verse.[2]

- *The Amplified Bible, Classic Edition* translates *Selah* as "pause and calmly think of, give thought to, consider that," pertaining to the preceding verse and the thought or truth it expressed.

Your story, very precious Reader, is different from mine. What is the same, though, is the love of God for you – He knows your own uniquely-created self, and what precisely will be life-giving hope for you alone. Some of the Words I share in *Learning to Be Loved* that brought me life may resonate with you, but you will also find others that are just for you alone. Know that He waits to encourage you with these Words!

His delight is to meet with, walk with, live every moment with you, His adored creation, inviting you to your own opportunities to *Selah* – to pause and consider, to teach you to hear His voice, to come know His character more fully. His character is rest, love, safety, peace, joy, goodness, kindness, tenderness, justice, and more. MUCH MORE!

My prayer is that you will be encouraged, tantalised, enthralled by His laughter and smile to reach out and take His hand and learn what it is for you to Be Loved.

Use A Journal

You may find it helpful to have a journal handy to note down various thoughts, feelings, and images that come to mind and heart as you read through *Learning to Be Loved*.

At the end of each chapter, I've included opportunities for your own **Selah** times, to **Pray the Word**, and to note some of Holy Spirit's **Breath of Life** rhema words that may stir your heart-ears to further listening.

Go Slow

Learning to Be Loved ~ Finding Your Way from Distressed to Rest is autobiographical in that it shares a piece of MY story, but it is also devotional and invitational, reaching out to you in YOUR story, offering opportunity to enter into and receive His gifts. As such, it is not a book to be rushed through, to be consumed in one sitting, or even in one week or month. Rather, it is best received slowly, a feast for the soul to be consumed one small bite at a time.

As I was writing *Learning to Be Loved*, praying always about how to present various themes, I found that on numerous occasions I would begin to write in a "stream of consciousness" poetic style. This actually surprised and delighted me! I saw it as a lovely gift of creative poetic voice being released, one of the many gifts just naturally brought forward by the healing I'd received! When you come upon these poems throughout the book, it is my hope and prayer that you will chew on them, consider, and slowly digest what has been birthed from Holy

Spirit's Breath in each place. I pray you will be encouraged toward your own unique hearing and expressing of our magnificent, marvelous God.

On That Note

Music is a love language for me! Throughout my life, music of wonderfully varying styles has underscored and furthered my experience and lens of seeing. To enrich your journey, in many of the activation portions of *Learning to Be Loved*, I've noted a piece of music that enhanced my receiving of the particular gem expressed. It looks like this:

> **On That Note ~**
> *We Dance* by Steffany Frizzell Gretzinger and Bethel Music

He's always putting a new song in my heart![3] I have found that He loves to dance, and His dance card is never full! He's always looking for willing partners.

> "Becoming the Beloved means letting the truth of our Belovedness become enfleshed in everything we think, say or do."[4]
>
> — HENRI NOUWEN

> *"The Lord your God is in the midst of you, a Mighty One, a Savior [Who saves]! He will rejoice over you with joy; He will rest [in silent satisfaction] and in His love He will be silent and make no mention [of past sins, or even recall them]; He will exult over you with singing!"*
>
> — ZEPHANIAH 3:17, AMPC

And Finally...

Dr. Mark Virkler, co-author of *4 Keys to Hearing God's Voice* with Patti Virkler, has very kindly shared a condensed version of his book in the Appendix of *Learning to Be Loved*. I urge you to take advantage of this gift, and also consider getting your own copy of his book. You can access some of his teachings online or receive even further teaching through Communion With God Ministries.[5] Dr. Virkler's whole desire is simply that people who hunger to hear God's voice can receive training on how to do so.

On This Side of It

It's difficult to remember (the suffocating weight,
    tears, fragility are gone
... yet I still know it's true):
what life was like before You gave me sight,
before You came into my numbed and terrored dark-
    ness, let me see Your face ...
and led me out.

Even after those early glorious revelation days,
    YEARS! all was not clear,
(for a while I thought it was...)
'til You in gentleness
allowed more to be seen,
revealing:
Pus of infection lying long hidden,
sealed deep within,
festering,
rising higher and closer
to the surface, threatening,
not to be ignored anymore,
ready for exposure, to be
seared with the Surgeon's white-hot scalpel Sword.
CLEANSED, then
comforted with Your Balm.

Years were lost
(I thought that was normal)
gaps in memory: short scenes only...
or what pictures prove took place.

Yet,
You took care of me,

even in the midst of my unknowing.

Though I did not know my value,
You did!

And You kept me through
Fears that roared and threatened,
Rage too,
Silence. A lot of silence.
Blurred Boundaries allowing in
what ought not to have been —
the fruit of not saying, not knowing how to say, not
    being ALLOWED to say,
NO!
Spiralling Depression stealing YEARS,
Gross images flashed frequently on mind's eye,
demonic night visitations,
Paralysis of
action,
of thought.
Numb.

Feeling responsible for ... EVERYTHING, everyONE,
And failing all.
Death's black promise of escape a frequent thought
    making
suicide a valid choice ...
including how, when and where
to accomplish it.

CONFUSION

and
Almost constant voices of

"Failure
FAILURE
Quitter
Worthless
Useless
STUPID,
only an Observer
with
Nothing to contribute.

A waste of skin."

I thought the voices were True.
I thought they were me (knowing indictment),

Until You came,

Bringing the Light that darkness hates,
Revealing the liar.

You brought Your Blood scarred hands, feet, side
saying, "Hands OFF!"
washing off every hell curse.

You've spoken:
Loved! Daughter! Gifted! Planned!
with a Destiny, a Purpose,
great Value!
That I am
Precious,
Creative,
and Little Pea too.
You named me
"My Delight is in you!"

You've smiled:
"Brilliant, Lovely, filled with
My Joy —
thus an able Warrior..."

You've whispered that I reflect Your Glory —
because I look so much at Your Face.

Pure.
Beloved.
Well.

And I am!
The well of tears is long gone.

— PART I —

WORDS of INVITATION

*"I am only a little rose or autumn crocus of the plain of
Sharon, or a humble lily of the valley ... You are My beloved!
Come away with Me!"*

Song of Songs 2:1,13, AMPC

1

THE LIVING WORD

"In the beginning was the Word....
and (He) was Life and Light."

John 1:1, 5, AMPC

"Your words were found and I ate them; and Your words
were to me a joy and the rejoicing of my heart..."

Jeremiah 15:16, AMPC

I love words! Words capture, intrigue, and fascinate me. They send me imagining. They speak depths and heights, creating and taking me beyond where I am. Words are infused with life—alive!

I love stories! I am fascinated by the stories of people's lives and what has been real for them, recognising each individual person's intrinsic and oh-so-interesting value!

And I love truth.

In March of 1980, during a fearful and low time in my life, I met the real Word, the true Word, the Living Word! I met the One Who knew and loved me from before the beginning, though I didn't know Him and have been slow to love back. I met the One Who spoke all of creation into being—that's how powerful words are! I met the One Who, as the Message translation of the Bible says in John 1, was birthed into human form and "moved into the neighbourhood."[1] I met the One Who, when we read Him, illuminates, examines, gets down to the nitty-gritty within, and tenderly convicts, heals, and divides between our breath-of-life soul and our immortal spirit. He is more finely sharpened than a two-edged sword, energising, examining, sifting, and penetrating: He is alive and full of power![2]

We've had a very special relationship of love since my ears were opened to recognise His voice all those years ago.

In the spring of 2013, I began to be taken through some of my own unremembered story, which was long awaiting the Light. The Word once made flesh, died and risen, again took my hand and led me into new territory. Over the course of the next five years, He spoke many life-giving words. He manifested the beauty, the gift, and the promise in each area as He restored my lost identity, releasing my lost voice. Along the way of writing this book, I was drawn into many instances of poetic response to His invitations. I hope you will find them meaningful as well, further opportunity for *Selah*.

A Surprise Invitation

"I see a little green pea, and it's in a green pea pod, and
it's floating down a river...
You are the pea!

Jesus is the pod!!
There's tall grass lining the edges of the water, and the
river is just flowing along – it's really safe.
And quiet.
And you don't have to do anything; you're simply being
carried – a pea in a pod."

This was spoken to me by a woman I did not know in the
spring of 2013. Only moments before, we had been introduced
to each other at an International School of Ministry (ILSOM)
hosted in Calgary, Alberta by Catch the Fire Toronto. We had
both asked Holy Spirit to quiet us as we listened for a
prophetic word or picture for the other, something to
encourage the other with, something from the Father heart
of God.

Thus began my journey into deeper intimacy with Jesus, the
One Who reveals the Father, the One Who loves, Who died His
sinless death to reconcile me (all!!) to my Father Who is Holy
Love; Jesus, the One Who rose that I may have new Life by His
Spirit — my Bridegroom, the Saviour-Lover of my soul. Thus
began my invitation into rest. The invitation is for you, too.

LITTLE PEA

*Just a little pea, last one in the pod, afloat on a gently
    flowing river
nothing to be done, no requirement, fear or folly
simply carried along,
one little pea.*

*Tall grass lines hidden banks, gently bowing o'er the
    water
undulating softly in hushed breeze.*

*Nothing seen beyond save blue sky and nearest
    corner,*
stillness is the sound that meets the ear.

*It's the ease that's most impactful, all taut striving
    vanished,*
little pea is just a pea within a pod.
There's no thought or need to be
other than a pea,
effortless and free,
released to simply BE
...a little pea.

*"Be still and rest in the Lord; wait for Him and patiently lean your-
self upon Him ..."*

— PSALM 37:37A, AMPC

2

SABBATICAL

*H*ave you ever had a sabbatical? Do you even know what it is? Isn't it for professors, or maybe pastors, or sometimes older folks seeking further knowledge, to take time away to focus on a particular subject, or be intent on higher learning? Don't you need to have money to do that? Doesn't it mostly take place in Europe? Isn't it for someone else, not related to me at all?

Sabbatical[1] (adjective)

- Of or pertaining or appropriate to the sabbath.
- Of or pertaining to a sabbatical year.
- Bringing a period of rest.

Sabbatical year[2] (noun)

- Any extended period of leave from one's customary work, especially for rest, to acquire new skills or training, etc.

- Also called sabbatical leave (in a school, college, university, etcetera); a year, usually every seventh, from release from normal teaching duties granted to a professor, as for study or travel.
- Chiefly Biblical; a yearlong period to be observed by Jews once every seven years, during which the fields were to be left untilled and all agricultural labors were to be suspended (Leviticus 25).

Though I've mostly been someone who did not put herself forward, I was strongly drawn to these folks from CTF Toronto who, for a season, birthed a gathering church in Calgary, Alberta where we lived. Although I was typically intimidated by anyone in leadership, feeling small and unworthy, with these CTF folks, I was eager to ask questions and learn from them. Rather than feeling intimidated, I felt almost compelled to come into relationship.

Both my husband, Grant, and I recognised the leading of God to get to know them and their experience of God better. But it was the most curious thing: almost every time I was with them, whether in large group gatherings or small, I would begin to cry. Emotions kept rising up, like a well of tears whose pump had been primed, and the water flowed non-stop! I didn't know why this was happening. There were just all these tears, seeming to come from a deep, hidden sorrow. One of the leaders commented early on that they suspected that God had brought me to a safe place to begin to recognise, release, and heal.

One day, at a small conference at another church, I clearly heard the strong whisper of God, saw it written out in large letters: "SABBATICAL."

I never knew how much terror I had in me, until I finally began to hear my Father's whispers (over and over, over and over), "Do not be afraid, little one, I've got you; I AM here." I never knew how much shame was within until I recognised that almost every time He spoke to me He said, "I will not ever shame you," and I came to see how shame had impacted almost every area of my life and choice and self-image. I never knew how much control I constantly tried to exert, until I heard, many times over, "You can let go now; I've got you; you are safe." I never knew how tired I was, how hard I had always been striving, until I began to hear, "Sabbatical... A Sabbatical year." And my heart cried: "Oh Yes. PLEASE!"

With tears.

A Sabbatical rest is a Sabbath rest and pertains to the Sabbath (the seventh day of creation), the day our Lord ceased His labours and said, "Fait accompli! It is soooooo good!!"

While "sabbatical" can refer to any period of time taken as rest, a "sabbatical year" is a year-long period of rest generally taken every seven years. Holy Lord of all, Creator of Heaven and earth, directed through Moses that it was in His creation's best interests to "remember the Sabbath and to keep it holy,"[3] for it is!

Our western world has largely lost the understanding and receiving of the Rest of the Sabbath of God. We've lost recognition that one of the most important gifts of our heritage is Rest, and that Sunday, the Sabbath, the first day of the week, was meant as an opportunity to be regularly intentional in rest: for quiet, a day for worship, for listening, for restoring balance to things that may have been knocked off centre, for recognising and receiving the "it is good" of God. And, if one can receive it, this rest is meant to be the foundation for ALL our days, not just one!

We've largely forgotten how to enjoy, how to play, how to live God's wonderful all-encompassing-forever: "Welcome to My Rest!!"

In Chapter 8 of his book *Spirit Wars,* Kris Valloton says,

> Remember when the Father said to Him (Jesus), "Sit at my right hand until I make your enemies a footstool for your feet" (Ps. 110:1)? Times like these (sitting times) remind me of ... Ps.23:2-3: "He makes me lie down in green pastures; He leads me beside quiet waters. He restores my soul." It is in these wonderful times that God teaches us about His love, mercy, and grace. I call these seasons "It's all about God" seasons. In these times, it seems that if I make any great efforts like trying to work hard, pray long or study diligently, that kind of messes it up. I know these are times that I am supposed to learn how to rest in God and how to trust Him with my entire life. ... It is in these "seated," all-about-God seasons that we learn how to live.[4]

> *"Are you tired? Worn out? Burned out on religion? Come to me. Get away with me and you'll recover your life. I'll show you how to take a real rest. Walk with me and work with me—watch how I do it. Learn the unforced rhythms of grace. I won't lay anything heavy or ill-fitting on you. Keep company with me and you'll learn to live freely and lightly!"*

> — MATTHEW 11:28-30, MSG

Activations For Learning to Be Loved

WORDS OF INVITATION

Breath of Life~

"Come up here. Come away with Me My fair one, My beloved. Come and sit with Me. Come and rest with Me, lean back into Me. Let yourself be carried—as a pea in a pod in the stream of Life—My very Living Waters, the place you are designed to be.

I will rest you, restore you, I will bring you to Life, alive and seeing from My wider viewpoint. You shall know My peace. You have been hearing the call to Cease striving, to be still, to rest... Finally you are hearing—Sabbatical rest—leaving off all. In this you hear it: Freedom!

And I will heal, quiet, and cleanse every area of fear, disability, and brokenness. I will make all your enemies a footstool under your feet, and you will rise in strength, whole, with a new calling and clear seeing. And you will carry My heart and walk in My authority and, in My Name, you will break chains of oppression that bind lives.

But for now, a season of sitting, of sabbatical *"an extended period of leave from one's customary work, especially for rest, and to acquire new skills or training."*

You will 'acquire new skills and training' as a natural outflow of resting in Me.
Your call is not to a Sabbatical year, but to a Sabbatical Life.

You are invited to My rest, My ceasing of labour, of work and striving, to My "It is good!"
You are called to Rest beloved! Always!
Be Loved. Live Loved!"

Selah ~

Has there been a deep, almost inexpressible, longing in your heart – you hardly know for what – just that you NEED A BREAK? Do you long to hear, have you begun to hear, Jesus calling; extending an invitation through many different sources: His Spirit's Breath, His Word, through teachers, books, friends, pictures and places, your own heart desperation?

Pray the Word ~

"O Jesus, I have been so very exhausted, burnt out, drained of life – I long for Your "unforced rhythms of grace."⁵ Teach me what it means to come to You, to bring You my needs, to live easy, freely, lightly: to rest."

3

REST, RESTORE, AND REFRESH

"...Don't you know he enjoys giving rest to those he loves?"

— PSALM 127:2B, MSG

*O*ur world, our lives, our every single moment, all seem to be moving at an ever-increasing rate of speed. There's often no time even for thinking, only for reacting, shoving off into the next frantic need-to-get-to thing screaming for our attention. Many of us feel as if we are all spinning out of control, screaming "Stop the world I want to get off! HELP!!!"

In 2013, I was feeling like I was on a mad hamster wheel, unable to break free of the cycle. God placed people in my life who kept speaking to me of my need for rest,[1] restoration,[2] and refreshing.[3]

Rest[4]

- (verb) Cease work or movement in order to relax, refresh oneself, or recover strength.
- Be placed or supported so as to stay in a specified position.
- Synonyms: lie, be laid, repose, be placed, be positioned, be supported by; e.g., "Her elbow was resting on the arm of the sofa" (a pea on a pod?!)

- (noun) An instance or period of relaxing or ceasing to engage in strenuous activity.
- Synonyms: repose, relaxation, leisure, respite, time off, breathing space, downtime.

Restore[5] (verb)

- To return something or someone to an earlier good condition or position;
- To bring back into use something that has been absent for a period of time;
- To give back something that has been lost or stolen.

Refresh[6] (verb)

- To revive or reinvigorate, as with rest, food, or drink;
- To renew by stimulation;
- To make cool, lean or moist: freshen up;
- To fill up again.
- Synonyms: reinvigorate, revitalize, revive, restore, fortify, enliven, perk up, stimulate, freshen, energize, exhilarate, reanimate, re-energize, wake up, revivify!

"The Lord is my Shepherd [to feed, guide, and shield me], I shall lack nothing. He makes me lie down in [fresh, tender] green pastures; He leads me beside the still and restful waters. He refreshes and restores my life (my self), (my soul)."

— PSALM 23:1-3A, AMPC, NIV, AMP

One day, I read those long-known verses and saw for the first time: "He RESTORES my SOUL." Cambridge Dictionary says this of *restore*: "If you restore a quality or ability that someone has not had for a long time, you make it possible for them to have that quality or ability again."[7]

WHAT??!! Wonder of wonders! I suddenly saw that I had a very false, ungodly belief (which many Christians hold), that the soul is selfish and should be denied. This belief was birthed in erroneous understanding of Jesus' instruction to "take up your cross, deny yourSELF daily and follow ME."[8] I believed the soul was nothing to pamper, something to be denied. But in the midst of very great exhaustion of body, mind and spirit, I heard God's whispers to step out of my many commitments, and instead to rest, rest, rest. And then, when fully rested, to enter in: to discovery, and welcome, and affirmation of all He made me to be.

Abba Father began speaking it so clearly, indeed more loudly than ever before (and He'd spoken it for years), promising that as I entered into what drew me most, that is where He would meet with me in fullness. Still, it took a long time to even begin to believe, to trust, and receive the grace and life of putting first in any day's plans what I'd always put last: what I actually wanted to do.

I began to hear many times over: "Follow your heart, for there I AM!" He even named *play* a "spiritual discipline" —more important than Biblical study, contemplation, prayer/intercessions, etcetera. For me, with my tendency to be OVERserious about what I consider important things and as one who likes clear directions, *play* is where He is revealing Himself! All those "disciplines" are only meant to be blessing and invitation to come into greater Revelation of the One Who loves after all!

I'm learning ever-so-slowly to let go of many walls of expectation of what He, and Life in Him, should look like. Rather, I am discovering Him as He IS ... as "I AM."

I AM your Healer.
I AM your Peace.
I AM your Shepherd.
I AM your Provision.
I AM your Friend.
I AM your Counsellor.
I AM your Advocate.
I AM your Refuge.
I AM your Helper.
I AM your Shield.
I AM your Strength.
I AM FOR you.
I AM your Father.
I AM your Saviour Redeemer.
I AM Merciful.
I AM Patient.
I AM Kind.
I AM full of Joy!
I AM your Secret Place.
I AM Life.
I AM your greatest Cheerleader!
I AM all you need.
and More...

These are words for those who are taskmasters over their own selves, having high expectations of performance, of giving all, ALL the time:

- those who see need in whatever form it takes and determine to meet it;
- those who take up the cross of exhaustion, of self-denial, of responding to the expectations of others;
- those who have few healthy boundaries for themselves or those around them,
- those whose depletion is complete.

He is *Good* and *Happy* and *Fun!* He is full of Life! He Laughs! and He is soooo Creative! No single expression can reveal Him fully—that's why we are all so diverse!

Activations For Learning to Be Loved

REST, RESTORE, AND REFRESH

Breath of Life ~

"I want to restore your soul, refresh your being. I want to show you who you are – all the riches within you that have been unfertilised, unwatered, squelched, buried, hidden deep, unknown, unrecognised and unaffirmed, all that has been sublimated, given up, intentionally resisted. I want to give you rest and refreshment – leading you beside very still and quiet waters, My easy paths, nourishing you as in fragrant fields of flowers, refreshing you with My Rain from heaven, My Living Waters of Life, so that you may begin to truly Live. Do what is easy – nothing more, for My yoke is easy and My burden is light! Give yourself the grace you give to others."

Selah ~

What has He been saying to you for forever that you have not been hearing? Where are your deaf and blind spots? What needs Rest, Restoring, Re-FRESHing?

Pray the Word ~

"*O my Father—forgive me for not understanding, not honouring who You have made me to be. I've been so slow to hear. I am exhausted from giving myself to many needs and there has been little joy for a long time. Thank You for calling me to Rest! Help me to discover what You mean when You speak of leading me to lie down in green pastures, restoring my soul by streams of quiet waters. Open the eyes of my understanding, that I may begin to see what You have for me.*"

4

CHOICE

I have always been extremely sensitive to the needs of others, particularly the ones few others seem to see. In this sensing/seeing, I have a heart response for each: to meet with, to help in any way possible, to serve, to somehow make their way easier. Therefore, it was almost inconceivable to NOT respond to need, to say NO to requests, and to set boundaries: boundaries that at this time needed to be VERY narrow, providing a sanatorium-oasis for my whole being, that I may begin to recover from years of over-extension (nobody's fault but my own!).

Choice[1] (noun)

- An act of selecting or making a decision when faced with two or more possibilities.

For years, every *Help Wanted* sign invoked sympathy for the need the business expressed and I wanted, felt almost compelled, to offer to fill it—every sign! Now that's out of balance.

Jesus told me I always have a choice.

In *The Artist's Way Every Day*, July 17, Julia Cameron writes:

> Charity begins at home" is not a bromide. It is a direction. It means start with being nice to yourself, your authentic self, then try being nice to everyone else. When we place ourselves too low in the pecking order, we feel henpecked and, yes, we feel peckish...When we undervalue ourselves, we literally bury ourselves in lives not our own.... When we stop playing God, God can play through us.[2]

This kind of fits well alongside "Love your neighbour as yourself" doesn't it? And the invitation to play... I began to say "No" to most of the perceived demands on my time.

" ... therefore, choose Life ..."

— DEUTERONOMY 30:19, AMPC

Activations For Learning to Be Loved

CHOICE

Breath of Life ~

"Learn to say 'no' even though some may not understand – I have called you to a sabbatical season and, if you can receive it, a sabbatical life.

I am intent on it – if you ignore the call, your very health will suffer greatly, mentally and physically, for you cannot long continue giving out of extremely reduced stores."

Selah ~

Did you know you have a choice every day? Every moment even? For Life or Death? For living free or living bound?

What do you need to trust God for? What do you need to say No to? What do you need to say Yes to?

Choose Life!

Pray the Word ~

Jesus, You surprise me. I've not thought of my choices as for Life or for Death. I need Your grace to recognise the difference between self-ishness, answering Your call to sacrificial living, and those things that are Life or Death to my very being. Awaken me to who You have made me to be and the choices I've made that have extinguished that flame of Life. Give me ears to hear Your voice!

5

SOAKING

*S*oaking, which is a term used to describe waiting quietly in God's presence, is a huge, fundamental value of the historical Church and many of God's people today. This is not a regimented, predetermined time (e.g., 5, 15, 30, 60 minutes or more) carved-out-of-the-day time for Bible reading, study, and heart-felt intercessions.

Soaking, as I came to learn, is intentional, invitational-to-Jesus quiet space where we can be loved by Him. In soaking time, as we give ourselves to Him, we in turn receive from Him: we become saturated, permeated in Holy Spirit of Living God, that He may become known to our being, down to our very core.

Soaking[1] (verb)

- To lie in and become saturated or permeated with (water or some other liquid);
- To pass, as a liquid, through pores, holes, or the like;
- To be thoroughly wet;
- To penetrate or become known to the mind or feelings.

He knows what we need, and He gives of Himself in those dry places, much like the rains falling on the dry ground in the desert, soaking into all its cracked fissures. And with this rain the beauty of the desert comes to life, with even the prickly cacti blooming incredible flowers and releasing fragrance. Just so, when we soak, still and quiet in God's presence, we become softened, refreshed by His Living Waters and soothed by His Balm. Old things become new, burdens are lifted, and answers to long-held questions have space to be heard. The water of heaven brings us to life and causes us to bloom, perfuming the atmosphere with the fragrance of Heaven.

In my call-to-rest season, long periods of lying in His stillness followed: inviting His Presence, often with quiet music underscoring the time set apart. Holy Spirit poured out the Living Waters of Life, drenching me in His Presence. I frequently saw myself floating in space or in a quiet pool, His waters of refreshing pouring over and through my being. It was incredibly soothing, always quieting. I could 'see' and feel much that was heavy being washed off my spirit, leaving me lighter, quiet, at rest.

One of my soaking quiet times birthed this awareness:

BEGINNINGS[2]

Your Kingdom is so quiet.

It just IS!
And so amazingly simple ...
Why does it seem so difficult to actually grasp!!?

O to be as a little child
who just accepts – knows no other response
simply receives,

taking love for granted!
Flourishing in freedom!

I'm getting younger every day though ~
with Your help;
spying new landscapes for exploring...

You keep lifting the veil higher
and I begin to see

———

"Be still, know I AM God."

— PSALM 46:10, NIV

*"Come to me, all you who are weary and burdened, and I will give
you rest."*

— MATTHEW 11:28, NIV

*"But those who wait upon God get fresh strength. They spread their
wings and soar like eagles, They run and don't get tired, they walk
and don't lag behind."*

— ISAIAH 40:31, MSG

"Be still before the Lord and wait patiently for him..."

— PSALM 37:7, NIV

"Wait for the Lord; be strong and take heart and wait for the Lord."

— PSALM 27:14, NIV

Activations For Learning to Be Loved

SOAKING

Selah ~

Does your heart long for His refreshing?

For all that is heavy to be washed off by pure Living Water, poured out from Heaven?

Have you positioned yourself to receive Him, invited His saturation?

On That Note ~

Soaking music possibilities:

- Alberto and Kimberly Rivera have a number of great soaking albums. Over the course of several months God used their *Draw Near* album to touch and heal me on a very deep level. Other Rivera albums for quiet soaking and upbuilding are *Peace*, *Captured*, *Dancing River*, and *Pneuma*.
- Julie True has many soaking albums that soothe the soul, lift up the spirit, and quiet the atmosphere. *Music*

to Journal By, Volume 1 and *Volume 2* are both particular favorites of mine.

- *Stillness: Piano Solos by Klaus*
- Terri Geisel solo piano albums

Pray the Word ~

"Jesus, I long for Your rest. Will You help me to quiet, to wait upon You, to trust You will meet me when I ask, to receive Your permeation of my being with Living Waters of refreshing? Your Word promises that as I wait quietly upon You, I will receive new strength, I will run and not be weary, and I will soar like the eagles! Thank You for Your promise of rest as I come to You. Here I am."

6

BREATHE ~ RESUSCITATE

*M*any times over the years and particularly preceding and through this season, I often felt like I was suffocating, that it was difficult to draw breath. Sometimes my breathing was so shallow it was barely there at all. It wasn't about asthma or any lung disease, it was disease of another kind, a disease of the heart – my depleted-of-life inner heart was barely taking up any space. My heart was in hiding.

BREATHE ON ME

My heart expression was
Devoid of life, lungs empty, almost flat
cells everywhere drying up...
Your CPR is needed or I die
a slow, painful
death
O come
O come Emmanuel
Breathe on me, in me, Breath of God!
O come!

"We breathe because oxygen is needed to burn the fuel [sugars and fatty acids] in our cells to produce energy. Oxygen is brought into the lungs via breathing, where it is transported by red blood cells to the entire body to be used to produce energy."[1]

Breath[2] (noun)

- The air taken into or expelled from the lungs;
- An inhalation or exhalation of air from the lungs;
- (archaic) The power of breathing; life, life force.

Resuscitate[3] (verb)

- To revive (someone) from unconsciousness or apparent death; bring back to consciousness; make active or vigorous again.
- Synonyms: revive, resurrect, restore, regenerate, revitalize, breathe new life into, reinvigorate, rejuvenate, stimulate.[4]

Holy Spirit is the Wind of God, the Breath of God, the *oxygen* of God that transports His very Life throughout our body, that we will be full of his energy, everything our lives need for Life; He is satisfying gulps of fresh air to every cell, invigorating. bringing fully alive!

*"Prophesy to these bones, and say to them, O you dry bones, hear the word of the LORD... Behold, **I will cause breath (and Spirit) to enter you, and you shall live**."*

— EZEKIEL 37:4-5, AMPC, EMPHASIS ADDED

"...on the first day of the week, when it was evening, though the
disciples were behind closed doors for fear of the Jews, Jesus came
and stood among them and said, Peace to you!So saying, He
showed them His hands and His side. And when the disciples saw
the LORD, they were filled with joy. Then Jesus said to them again,
Peace to you! Just as the Father has sent Me forth, so I am sending
you. And, having said this, **He breathed on them and said to them:
Receive the Holy Spirit!**"

— JOHN 20:19-22, AMPC, EMPHASIS ADDED

Activations For Learning to Be Loved

BREATHE

Selah ~

Have you ever felt that it's difficult to breathe? that you are living a suffocated life? That your whole being needs CPR? Do your lungs long for Breath?

On That Note ~

I Breathe You In, God by Brian & Katie Torwalt

Pray the Word ~

"Dear Jesus, thank You for Your Word assuring me it is Your desire for me to be full of Your Breath. I so often feel devoid of life. I want to Live! Just like Your disciples, I need YOUR Life in me – will You come, breathe on me, in me, fill my dry bones, my lungs, and my being with Your fresh Wind. Holy Spirit, I invite You: teach me how to breathe You deep, every day, every moment."

7

CEASE STRIVING

*H*oly Spirit began to speak "cease striving" more and more frequently. At times it was just a whisper, with the sense of His loving smile, but other times it was louder and stronger. Sometimes I saw CEASE STRIVING in big capital letters in my mind's eye or written in the sky in front of me like a SHOUT! It happened so often that I knew He was helping me to be consciously aware of how deeply it was ingrained to feel the need to try to control EVERYTHING in my world.

Striving[1] (verb)

- To exert oneself vigorously; try hard;
- To make a strenuous effort toward any goal;
- Or, great and tenacious efforts to do something.[2]

He slowly pulled back the layers, allowing me to see that my striving was about performance (which actually could never measure up). And He gave grace to begin to understand that it was also about fear, and control, and safety – before I knew there was a *reason* that I felt fear and such desperate need for control and safety.

He often whispered, "In quietness and in trust is your strength."[3] Sounds easy right? It is...but it's not.

There can be so many layers to un-layer in us. We develop built-in responses, and we don't understand why we do or say the things we do. We fall into patterns, developing deeply worn ruts of long-lived behavior. We develop places of unbelief and fear, longing for rest but sabotaging opportunities, creating defenses that prevent us from trusting or receiving.

*"Let be and be still, **Cease Striving** and know (recognize and understand) that I am God."*

— PSALM 46:10, AMPC, NASB, EMPHASIS
ADDED

*"For he who has once entered [God's] rest also has ceased from [the weariness and pain] of human labors, just as God rested from those labors] peculiarly His own. Let us therefore be zealous and exert ourselves and **strive diligently to enter that rest [of God, to know and experience it for ourselves,** that no one may fall or perish by the same kind of unbelief and disobedience [into which those in the wilderness fell]."*

— HEBREWS 4:10-11, AMPC, EMPHASIS
ADDED

Activations For Learning to Be Loved

CEASE STRIVING

Breath of Life ~

"My precious one, I invite you into My rest – how I love you!

How you make Me smile! How I long for you to know the completeness of My Rest, My Peace, in every cell of your being.

I have more, so much more, than you could ever guess is possible. I have known you from before your beginning; and I AM bringing you refreshment and life, restoring the goodness of My desire for you and everything which has been lost.

I AM bringing rejuvenation with an energy that is vital and alive, not forced, or compelled, but freely, easily, joyfully, even exuberantly given!

You can let go now.

Strive only to enter My rest!

Your being needs re-plenishing – let Me plenish you!"

Selah ~

Do you recognise some of those same things in yourself? The need, the compulsion for perfection, to direct EVERYTHING? to feel you know the best for any situation and therefore you have to tell everyone the "correct" way (for their own benefit of course)?

Do you recognise patterns of insecurity, pushing beyond your limits, resentment, or longing to somehow not have to do it all?

"Strive diligently to enter rest" – a conundrum if there ever was one! Must be something to chew on...or pray.

Pray the Word ~

"Ah, Father – once again I see Your invitation to rest – the rest You began on the seventh day of creation and clearly mean for Your beloveds, for me, to live in constantly! Help me see the places I enter into striving to make things happen, instead of listening for Your quiet directing, for what is my part – easy and light. Help me to know what it means to 'strive diligently to enter' Your rest."

8

REPLENISH

his calling to Sabbatical time – God's call to soak, rest, quiet – allowed me to see that my distress at every new need (whether regular daily doings around the home or, more particularly, someone else's request for time) was because I had nothing left in my tank.

Replenish[1] (verb)

- To fill something up again, restore (a stock of supply of something) to its former level or condition.

Just as a vehicle cannot run when the gas tank is empty, neither could I. I'd been running on empty for a long time; the pattern I'd followed in the past of spending time with Jesus in the morning then going about the day, just wasn't enough. This time called for a thorough restocking, a "closed for maintenance" sign, to allow for a complete overhaul.

"For I will [fully] satisfy the weary soul, and I will replenish every languishing and sorrowful person."

— JEREMIAH 31:25, AMPC

*Jesus said, "...Anyone who drinks the water I give will never thirst —not ever. **The water I give will be an artesian spring within, gushing fountains of endless life!**"*

— JOHN 4:14, MSG, EMPHASIS ADDED

Activations For Learning to Be Loved

REPLENISH

Breath of Life ~

"be.

a pea.

in a pod.

carried.

and I will fill you with Myself,

replenishing,

refilling

refueling

all the depleted stores of your being."

Selah ~

Are the shelves of your supply room empty?

Could you use some replenishing right now?

Do you need to be restocked?

Pray the Word ~

"Father, thank You that You know me. You know my weariness, the languishing, even sorrow within. Thank You that You not only know my thirst but have gushing fountains of the Living Water of Jesus to replenish my soul as I take conscious time to be in Your Presence, to receive Your 'restocking of the shelves' of my life."

9

LOVE

*O*xford Dictionary defines "love" as "an intense feeling of deep affection... fondness, tenderness, warmth, intimacy, attachment, endearment, compassion, care, caring, regard, solicitude, concern, warmth, friendliness, friendship, kindness, charity, goodwill, sympathy, kindliness, altruism, philanthropy, unselfishness, benevolence..."[1]

Have you imagined, hoped for, cried out for, only dreamt about (as seeming impossible), a love like that? Have you just about given up on finding it?

We human beings have great capacity and longing for "true love." Witness all the romantic movies, poems, songs, and stories, as well as the difficulties encountered as the characters discover the challenging limitations and disappointments engendered by human love. This includes (if we are honest) our own limited-in-love selves. Many tears have been shed over broken relationships, betrayals, failure, and the lost hope of truly being loved.

My heart has long loved my Father, Papa God. I have SO loved sitting at His feet or being held as in His arms, listening, resting in His quiet, and having my love returned. I have always loved loving Him, and for almost thirty-five years had expressed incredible longing to be so full of His presence that He (in me) would be life wherever I go. I only wanted Him to be seen, known, and received in His goodness. I'd been discovering the width and height and depth and breadth and length of His love in its fullness through all these years.[2]

But, He softly said many times, we cannot give away to others what we do not have ourselves: experience of that wide broad love that nothing can break or bring to an end.

There is always MORE to receive.

We are invited to, we get to, we must each receive the FULLness of His love before we can genuinely love ourselves or anyone else, before we can truly give love away.

Many times, I have had to repent of unbelief – that a love so great is possible, is mine, but...

> *Oh! Oh! Oh!*
> *when those glimmers of seeing, sensing come!*
> *Oh! Oh! Oh!*
> *I am undone!*
> *And caught up, into a taste of heaven.*

"May Christ through your faith [actually] dwell (settle down, abide, make His permanent home) in your hearts! May you be rooted deep in love and founded securely on love,

That you may have the power and be strong to apprehend and grasp with all the saints [God's devoted people, the expe-

rience of that love] what is the breadth and length and height and depth [of it];

[That you may really come] to know [practically, through experience for yourselves] the love of Christ, which far surpasses mere knowledge [without experience];that you may be filled [through all your being] unto all the fullness of God [may have the richest measure of the divine Presence, and become a body wholly filled and flooded with God Himself]!"

— EPHESIANS 3:17-19, AMPC

"We love because He first loved us."

— 1 JOHN 4:19, NASB

"He brought me to the banqueting house, and his banner over me was love [for love waved as a protecting and comforting banner over my head when I was near him]."

— SONG OF SOLOMON 2:4, AMPC

"He pastures his flocks among the lilies."

— SONG OF SONGS 2:16, AMPC

"The Lord is my shepherd, I lack nothing. He makes me lie down in green pastures, he leads me beside quiet waters, he refreshes my soul. He guides me along the right paths for his name's sake. Even though I walk through the darkest valley, I will fear no evil, for you are with me; your rod and your staff, they comfort me. You prepare a table before me in the presence of my enemies. You anoint my head with oil; my cup overflows. Surely your goodness and

love will follow me all the days of my life, and I will dwell in the house of the Lord forever."

— PSALM 23, NIV

Activations For Learning to Be Loved

LOVE

Breath of Life ~

"I love to be with you, to draw you further and further
into rest that your whole being may be in peace. This is
why I came ~ that all My Father's creation would walk
and live always with Him in refreshment and enjoyment, conversing, gesticulating, trying new things,
discovering, and celebrating together eternally, no end,
in peace, in such rest of heart and mind, soul and spirit,
that there is not even a second's quiver of concern.

You are My beloved – all are My beloved if they will
believe it! I know and love you as none other knows and
loves you, and in Me you truly do have ALL you will
ever, ever need.

I will always give you green pastures to rest and refresh
in – full of nourishment and richness, soft to find repose
in, safe;
I will always lead you by still and quiet waters of
refreshment and restore your soul completely – no
matter where you are – even in the presence of enemies

and great evil; I will provide for you in abundance, amazingly well, even in joy!

I will always anoint your head, your being, with the oil of My Spirit and your cup of blessing and My Presence will overflow and touch many. My oil will be soothing balm, warm, saturating, all for your own self and to give away — all encompassing.

I will lead and guide you always.
You have entered into My home – My Father's heart – and this is where you shall live forever! Explore all the rooms and passageways for surely they are full of goodness, mercy, every good thing – indeed, all you shall ever need.

Be at peace My beloved, for surely I love you with an everlasting love; I have drawn you and will keep you always with unfailing kindness!"

"There is nothing you need to do – to see Me, to know Me, to gain wisdom, to let creativity come forth and flow, to hear My voice.
Nothing – save rest.
Rest in My love.
I require nothing.
I only want to release you from all the pressure of trying to figure things out, to "get it right," to respond "correctly."

You are well. I have made you well! You are Mine!
I AM bringing an end to the 'doing', to restore *being* ~ in

restful relationship with your Father, to walk in the garden with Him in the cool and quiet of the day, filling with joy – deep, sound, all-encompassing, life-giving, heretofore-unknown-in-this-world-since-the-fall (except by those who have caught glimpses of, and have become My prophets of) joy!

You have no idea how great and wide and high and deep and broad and long My love is for you, for My creation, for all!

I want to rest you in the fullness of all My love and My smile, My Life-giving Presence. It is Who I AM!
I want to wash your mind of all stress and strain of trying to see and figure out and "do."
I want to wash you of all condemnation, of 'shoulds' and requirements, of fear of failure, of rejection, of sorrow, of loss.

Eye has not seen, nor heart understood what I have in store for those who love Me.[3]
I always have more for you - more abundantly than you can ask or imagine![4]

I love you – I knit you together in your mother's womb; I gave you all your special proclivities[5] – those things that make you YOU - one of a kind!
I have not created you to disappoint you but to rather bring you into the fullness of all our Father has for the colourful expression of His Kingdom—His Love— through you.

And you shall be more than well!"

Selah ~

Have you heard His whisper of adoration for you? Would you like to?

Consider: have you doubted your worth? Or the truth of the love of God? Or your ability to receive?

Is your heart quickened in hope, in longing? Will you dare to believe Love?

On That Note ~

Song of Solomon by Martin Smith & Jesus Culture

Reckless Love by Cory Asbury & Bethel Music

It is Well by Bethel Music, with Kristene DiMarco

Pray the Word ~

"O God, I long to know the fullness of Your love. Help me to recognise Your expressions and acts of love for me. Thank You that You want me to know the wide, deep, high, broad length of the fullness of the love of Jesus! Thank You that You cover and protect me, that Your banner of love is over my life, that You are my Shepherd and in You I lack nothing! I am amazed that You desire to feed my being in all manner of lovely ways, that You have refreshing streams for me to be revived by. Your love is meant to restore me, guide me, and even in the midst of darkness and trouble You promise me a feast of Your Presence and provision. Thank You."

10

COMING HOME

$\mathscr{I}$n pondering the wide expanse of the love of Abba Father and all He had been speaking and inviting me into, the story of what has long been known as *The Prodigal Son* in Scripture came to mind. I felt prompted to look up the word *prodigal*, and suddenly I viewed this story in a different way.

Prodigal[1] (noun)

- Wastefully or recklessly extravagant; prodigal expenditure;
- Giving or yielding profusely; lavish;
- Lavishly abundant; profuse.

It came to my awareness that, instead of being called *The Prodigal Son*, a better title may be *The Prodigal Father...* or, at the very least, *The Prodigal Son and his Prodigal Father*.

THE PRODIGAL SON AND HIS PRODIGAL FATHER

A prodigal child: I've been one: wastefully or reckless-
ly extravagant,
giving or yielding profusely; lavish,
though I did not have riches to squander...that is,
except myself.
A prodigal Father: My Dad IS one: giving or yield-
ing profusely; lavishly abundant; profuse.

"Jesus continued: "There was a man who had two sons. The younger one said to his father, 'Father, give me my share of the estate.' So he divided his property between them.

Not long after that, the younger son got together all he had, set off for a distant country and there squandered his wealth in wild living. After he had spent everything, there was a severe famine in that whole country, and he began to be in need. So he went and hired himself out to a citizen of that country, who sent him to his fields to feed pigs. He longed to fill his stomach with the pods that the pigs were eating, but no one gave him anything.

When he came to his senses, he said, 'How many of my father's hired servants have food to spare, and here I am starving to death! I will set out and go back to my father and say to him: Father, I have sinned against heaven and against you.

I am no longer worthy to be called your son; make me like one of your hired servants.' So he got up and went to his father. But while he was still a long way off, his father saw him and was filled with compassion for him; he ran to his son, threw his arms around him and kissed him.

The son said to him, 'Father, I have sinned against heaven and against you. I am no longer worthy to be called your son.' But the father said to his servants, 'Quick! Bring the best robe and put it on him. Put a ring on his finger and sandals on his feet. Bring the fattened calf and kill it. Let's have a feast and celebrate. For this son of mine was dead and is alive again; he was lost and is found.'

So they began to celebrate!"

— LUKE 15:11-24, NIV

ON BEING PRODIGAL AND COMING HOME

So we see it is possible to be prodigal – wastefully
      extravagant with things of value–
(like money, time, me)
expending huge quantities of what is precious
and ending with pig slop,
with no sustaining nutrients at all.

but it's not the word or action that's wrong
(as I always thought)
– prodigal –
it's the uses!
it's the motive underneath!
and when you have endless supply
(like my Father)
it's not really extravagance at all,
it's just
right.

Boy oh boy does He like to celebrate His kids!
Parties are big on His list of enjoyments
because He spends a lot of time

facing outward
watching
looking
for just one turn of the head
heart
toward Home ...
and then He's RUNNING TO MEET the one who
    thought they knew what they wanted
'til they didn't
and He celebrates
with JOY!
never never a word of recrimination
just,
Oh man, I'm SO GLAD YOU'RE HOME!

An old renovating commercial had a jingle, "Why wait for spring? Do it now!" Why wait—thrill God's heart and come home.

Activations For Learning to Be Loved

COMING HOME

Selah ~

Have you been squandering your precious self on things that are not life-giving?

Come home to a Father Who only waits to love you extravagantly. Come Home to His heart.

Do it now!

Pray the Word ~

"O God – O FATHER – Thank You. You have let me see that my own self is the precious treasure that I squander when I resist You, turn my back on You like a spoiled child, and stomp out of Your house, thinking my own way is better. Thank You for not turning Your back on me, but instead watching and waiting, waiting for the day I would turn to come Home. Thank You for running to meet me, for giving me a place at Your table in celebration, clothing me in Your best robe mantles, and identifying me as one of Your own. I thought I deserved to be left on the periphery, looking on, but instead, You gave me You! I never want to leave Home again, so help me to stay right

near You—held, celebrated, taught, known. Grow me in under-standing all that it means to be Your loved child."

— PART II —

WORD LESSONS from PIP

*"My prayer is that light will flood your hearts
and that you will understand the hope that was given to you
when God chose you. Then you will discover the glorious
blessings that will be yours
together with all of God's people."*

Ephesians 1:18, CEV

11

SAFETY

Our Pip (short for Pipsqueak—so named because her meows were mere high-pitched squeaks) came to us from the Humane Society in 2010. Her estimated age was one year at the time. She was quite beautiful, though rather cross-looking, and her long, almost-black coat with white markings was the softest shiniest hair ever, softer than silk.

She was chosen for several reasons. I've always had cats and for quite a few years more than one at a time. When Pip came home to live with us we only had our big brown tabby, Frodo, who was a lounge-around, huggy kind of guy. We (myself and husband Grant, who has had no choice but to become a cat... lover? tolerator?) thought it would be good to save another cat from the noise, trauma and sadness of not being chosen at the SPCA and to find a friend and playmate for Frodo.

Being black, Pip was chosen because I'd read that black cats get chosen less; and also she reminded me somewhat of my long-ago Kitty that I grew up with and loved desperately until he was cruelly poisoned by a neighbour (another story) at the ripe old age of sixteen.

Pip didn't enjoy being held (slight understatement!), but I figured I could love her into it as we'd done with our previous kitty Sasha, who took over three years to become comfortable with being close.

Pip was soft and very precious; in fact, we almost named her Precious, but because we already had a Frodo, we didn't want people thinking we were overdoing it with Lord of the Rings allusions. Then we completely disregarded that very reasoning in choosing the name Pip, even though Frodo's friend Pippin in Tolkein's trilogy could garner us the same recognition – but our Pip was PipSQUEAK after all!

Upon being introduced to our home and Frodo (having read of slow introductions being helpful for both felines), we kept Pip in our bedroom for a few days with her own supply of food and litter, which we placed in our ensuite bathroom - it was her own safe space. Little did we know that this cosy little area on our thick, rosy-red bath mat would imprint into her as her one safe, sheltered, happiest place in our whole home. Now, many years later, when I enter my bedroom she often runs from out of nowhere to try and lure me to the bathroom, meowing (squeaking, squawking), willing me to come and stroke and brush her on the rosy bathmat.

She's an entirely different kitty when she's comfortable and safe...she can let her hair down.

Safety[1] (noun)

- The state of being safe; freedom from the occurrence or risk of injury, danger, or loss.

Like Pip, I am entirely different when I do not feel threatened. I too have found my safe place, the place where I can "let my hair down" and be real; where I am hidden, known, cherished, encouraged, comforted, celebrated, laughed with, inspired, stabilised, taught, loved, completely at ease, and utterly well. The most extraordinary thing about my place of safety – the secret place of the Most High[2] – is that it is not a physical location like a red bath mat, or nature, or a church building, or even a quiet space. My safe place is in my Father's HEART and He is anywhere I am – where I am, He IS![3] No more needing prayer closets, or to get to a certain location, or to fight frantic fears alone – He is always present!

Here I AM

Moments ago, wallowing in torment
You are always whispering (when I cry out Where
*   are You??):*

"Here I AM!
I AM here!"

Here You ARE
Your Resurrected Life HERE
tender, quiet, powerful,
being shelter
hiding me in You

You surround me, You hold me, Your broad back
*   blocking the waves from crashing on me,*
inviting me into Truth: You are in Your holy temple ...
*   me...!!*
And all the earth must hush, be SILENT before You.
Truth comes again. I am well.

"You are a hiding place for me; You, Lord, preserve me from trouble, You surround me with songs and shouts of deliverance. Selah [pause, and calmly think of that]!"

— PSALM 32:7, AMPC

"He who dwells in the secret place of the Most High shall remain stable and fixed under the shadow of the Almighty [Whose power no foe can withstand]. I will say of the Lord, He is my Refuge and my Fortress, my God; on Him I lean and rely, and in Him I [confidently] trust!"

— PSALM 91:1-2, AMPC

"The name of the Lord is a strong tower; The righteous run to it and are safe."

— PROVERBS 18:10, NKJV

"I will answer your cry for help every time you pray, and you will find and feel my presence even in your time of pressure and trouble. I will be your glorious hero and give you a feast. You will be satisfied with a full life and with all that I do for you. For you will enjoy the fullness of my salvation!"

— PSALM 91:15-16, TPT

Activations For Learning to Be Loved

SAFETY

Breath of Life ~

"I'm HERE! Lay your head upon Me, I hold you in My heart. My Peace be your Peace, My Joy, your Joy! I hide you in Me, Precious Pea."

Always safe, always known, always led, always loved.
Even in the very midst of cacophony and chaos
His enveloping heart is Peace.

Selah ~

Have you longed for a place of safety where you can just be you, no masks, no faking it?

You too are invited to meet with God in His secret place; to dwell, live, abide always, in His Presence, in His heart.

Take some time to voice your longing. Consider His promises: what does "His faithfulness is your shield and buckler" mean for you?

On That Note ~

You Make Me Brave by Amanda Cook and Bethel Music

Pray the Word ~

"Father, thank You for Your invitation to be hidden in Your secret place, for your promise to keep me safe there, for letting me see that learning to make my home in Your heart will bring me stability, shelter, and strength. I need Your help to even begin to believe that kind of love. Thank You for promising to be my refuge in times of trouble, that You are faithful, and You surround me just like a shield – protected always! Thank You for hearing me whenever I cry out, for wanting me to know You, that Your desire for me is an abundant, full, satisfied life!

Thank You for being my refuge, my hiding place! Thank You that I can run to You always and be safe – let me hear Your shouts of victory and deliverance that You surround me with, that I may begin to join in, and shout my victory too!"

12

VULNERABILITY

*G*etting to know Pip has been a journey, not necessarily an easy one. It has required us to be intentional in learning her own particular quirks and to not close off against her because she has really not been very snuggly at all, which was my primary reason for wanting a cat!

Pip frightens easily. She is rarely at rest when there is anyone in the room, quick to jump and flee at any sudden movement or noise, tearing off out of the room or as far down the hallway as possible. She will seldom sit near anyone for long. But she also craves interaction, presence, and closeness – under her own terms of course.

This can be a particular corner of a particular couch at a particular time of day (it all changes regularly), and she will squeak, squeak, SQUAWK (Pipsqueak Pipsquawk!) to get you to come sit beside her where she will immediately wrap one hind leg over your arm that you may rub her tummy! And she can receive that kind of loving for five to ten minutes! Or some days, one minute.

Pip has a story, her beginnings unknown. She was a pregnant one-year-old when the Humane Society took her in. They aborted the litter and spayed her to prepare her for adoption. Who knows what scary stuff took place in her life prior to us meeting her, what bad treatment, what terror and trauma? I've often wondered if the compulsion to have her tummy rubbed comes from muscle/brain memory of a litter that never came to fruition?

But after about seven years Pip began to oh-so-slowly open up, long after lumbering Frodo died. She was slowly relaxing, showing brief enjoyment, sometimes even waiting close by the door for us to come home...it took time.

Vulnerability[1] (noun)

- The state of being vulnerable or exposed, susceptible to injury or attack.

Aren't we all Pips to one degree or another? With stories not fully known, not even to ourselves? With reactions that can seem ridiculous, unnecessary, and way over the top; or with peculiarities and penchants that seem unexplainable, perhaps lovable and precious, or odd, even daft - with extreme caution protecting our vulnerable places – sometimes wanting those old wounds massaged with attention, many of them so deeply hidden we don't even know they are there?

Doesn't our Holy Dad exercise His great love and long-suffering patience as He invites us in to Love? HE knows He is safe, that He has so much good, health and life for us that we don't even know is a possibility, let alone His laughing eager destiny for us. But He doesn't push: He woos, responding quietly to our own erratic, contradictory behaviours as we alternately long for Him yet run from Him for reasons we cannot explain or understand.

"I have loved you with an everlasting love, and drawn you with unfailing kindness!"

— JEREMIAH 31:3, NIV

"Therefore the Lord waits [expectantly] and longs to be gracious to you, And therefore He waits on high to have compassion on you. For the Lord is a God of justice; Blessed (happy, fortunate) are all those who long for Him [since He will never fail them]."

— ISAIAH 30:18, AMP

Activations For Learning to Be Loved

VULNERABILITY

On That Note ~

You Know Me by Steffany Frizzell Gretzinger and Bethel Music

Selah ~

Do you know where you are vulnerable, what you don't want anyone to see? Are there wounds within compelling you to reactions that you don't understand? Would you like to whisper an invitation to the One Who Loves, give Him permission to bring His love to what hurts?

Pray the Word ~

"Father, You already know everything about me. Thank You for being patient with me, thank You for Your kindness towards me, for Your love from FOREVER and for ALWAYS that is frequently more than I understand or know how to receive. You long to be gracious to me - please help me to trust You, to invite You into where it hurts, instead of shying away. I make Psalm 139:1-18 (MSG) my prayer..."

"God, investigate my life; get all the facts firsthand. I'm an open book to you; even from a distance, you know what I'm thinking. You know when I leave and when I get back; I'm never out of your sight. You know everything I'm going to say before I start the first sentence.

I look behind me and you're there, then up ahead and you're there, too—your reassuring presence, coming and going. This is too much, too wonderful—I can't take it all in! Is there any place I can go to avoid your Spirit? to be out of your sight? If I climb to the sky, you're there! If I go underground, you're there! If I flew on morning's wings to the far western horizon, You'd find me in a minute— you're already there waiting!

Then I said to myself, "Oh, he even sees me in the dark! At night I'm immersed in the light!" It's a fact: darkness isn't dark to you; night and day, darkness and light, they're all the same to you. Oh yes, you shaped me first inside, then out; you formed me in my mother's womb. I thank you, High God—you're breathtaking!

Body and soul, I am marvellously made! I worship in adoration— what a creation! You know me inside and out, you know every bone in my body; You know exactly how I was made, bit by bit, how I was sculpted from nothing into something. Like an open book, you watched me grow from conception to birth; all the stages of my life were spread out before you, The days of my life all prepared before I'd even lived one day.

Your thoughts—how rare, how beautiful! God, I'll never comprehend them! I couldn't even begin to count them—any more than I could count the sand of the sea. Oh, let me rise in the morning and live always with you!"

13

ANYTHING FOR LOVE

*B*ecause I dearly want Pip to know she is loved and enjoy it, to know she is safe, that she can trust me, to be peaceful in our home and free to be restful; because I love her, I choose to allow her to interrupt me often. Whether I'm praying, reading, writing, cleaning, or getting ready for whatever, I want her to know that my heart is for her, that she is important, she matters, and I would love to see her wholly happy!

I want her to know she can trust me.

Sacrifice[1] (verb)

- To sacrifice is to give up something that is important to you in order to help another.

Of course, there are also many times that I cannot and do not give in to her attempts to get my attention – when I'm sleeping! when I have much to do! when I'm baking! if she is angry and disagreeable, when I don't want to be interrupted, and of course, when I'm not even there.

WHAT LOVE LOOKS LIKE

Clearly, there are limits to my love.
Unlike our Father Who is always present, never
  sleeps,
Who withholds nothing good from His beloveds.
EVER,
Whose ear is always open to our cry...
I've a ways to go in love....
What our Father's Love looks like:
"...God gave His only Son..." (John 3:16, NIV).

———

"... when the time was right, the Anointed One came and died to demonstrate his love for sinners who were entirely helpless, weak, and powerless to save themselves. Now, who of us would dare to die for the sake of a wicked person? We can all understand if someone was willing to die for a truly noble person. But Christ proved God's passionate love for us by dying in our place while we were still lost...!"

— ROMANS 5:5-8, TPT

Activations For Learning to Be Loved

ANYTHING FOR LOVE—SACRIFICE

On That Note ~

Love on the Line by Hillsong Worship

Selah ~

How about you? Do you have limits on gifting love? Have you resisted dying for anyone recently, especially one who appears quite undeserving? Do YOU feel undeserving?

Pray the Word ~

"O Father – Your love encompasses all! Thank You that Your love has no limits, as mine does. Thank You that You held nothing back to display Your love for Your creation. Help me to recognise the extent of Your sacrifice for me, even giving Your beautiful Son Jesus to be sacrifice in my place, that I may be restored to relationship with You."

14

PERSISTENCE, PART 1

*a*s she grew a little more comfortable with love and more confident that I would respond to her, my oh my, how Pip began to make her needs and preferences known! She used to be pretty silent, just little squeaks of expression now and then, but after Frodo died—it took Pip two years!—she became increasingly demanding, often very loudly and persistently.

Persistence[1] (noun)

- Firm or obstinate continuance in a course of action in spite of difficulty or opposition.

And I think it's because she learned she can get results! We have to respond to her. She is part of the family: she gets to make her needs known! Because I promised the Humane Society years ago that I would take care of her, I signed my name to the pact (though not in blood).

I am responsible for her; she is valued and loved.

She's finally believed the proof of that.

Coming to believe we are loved opens up all kinds of possibilities. We have a relationship we can count on and that we can go to in any need; a relationship that shelters and protects, loves, guides and provides, because our Father loves, because He signed His Name for us on the legal documents of Heaven and Earth in the Blood of His Son.[2] This *knowing* is a very solid and secure place from which to live.

Our young grandson has been an excellent teacher of what it is to ask in child-like faith. He has no qualms about making his needs known! It's all about him! Center of attention!

We are invited to come to our own Abba Father as a child – He waits for us to persist in coming to Him for every need:

> *"Consider the incredible love that the Father has shown us in allowing us to be called "children of God"—and that is not just what we are called, but what we are."*

> — 1 JOHN 3:1, PHILLIPS

> *"Ask and keep on asking and it will be given to you; seek and keep on seeking and you will find; knock and keep on knocking and the door will be opened to you.*

> *For everyone who keeps on asking receives, and he who keeps on seeking finds, and to him who keeps on knocking, it will be opened. Or what man is there among you who, if his son asks for bread, will [instead] give him a stone?"*

> — MATTHEW 7:7-10, AMP

Activations For Learning to Be Loved

PERSISTENCE

Selah ~

Did you know you are absolutely invited to be part of the best, most loving, supportive family on earth, in the galaxy and BEYOND? What may you find confidence to persist in bringing before your Father based on THAT?!! What "bread" (sustenance, need, provision, starved-soul hunger) may you ask for?

Pray the Word ~

"Wow, Father! Not just a word, but a relationship – You are my Father, I am Your child! Thank You for Your incredible love! Teach me what it means to be a child of God. Thank You for giving me the "rights" of that relationship - that I can count on Your provision of all I need – food, wisdom, shelter, direction, grace, Your very Presence. Thank You for Your promise that as I ask and keep on asking – just like a 3 year old – I will receive Your best for me, that as I seek You and Your Kingdom, I will find You, that as I keep knocking on the door of heaven, You will open to me all that I hunger for."

15

PERSISTENCE, PART 2

*T*here is another kind of persistence we are called to: to keep going forward, one step at a time, choosing to not stop, and not to give up.

Pip did it, I think; at the very least she was forced to. After whatever happened in her early life: somehow being caught and taken to the SPCA, caged, surrounded by noise and mayhem, enforced surgery(!) and, finally, after who-knows-how-many strangers coming near, touching her, picking her up (which she hates), and finally being taken to another new place with another cat in charge and a giant dog too...fear!

Yet Pip kept on. Self-protective, yes; reacting prickly, yes; but finding some good things about this new location too; hiding much, long tentative, but finally responding, more and more, to love.

There was a period over several years when quite a number of people (some I hadn't known until moments before) took my hands, looked into my eyes, and said, "Keep going forward, take one step, take another step. Keep going, one step at a time."

I have been reminded of that frequently, particularly when things feel really tough and I am tempted to go back to bed and pull the covers over my head, to give up – but then the whisper, quietly encouraging, that I only need to take the next step in front of me, not do what seems the looming impossible whole.

Our Dad Who loves encourages us forward, always with a purpose for healing, wholeness, redemption, and life. He knows our "pregnant condition," and what He is bringing to birth.

> *"Meanwhile, the moment we get tired in the waiting God's Spirit is right alongside helping us along. If we don't know how or what to pray, it doesn't matter. He does our praying in and for us, making prayer out of our wordless sighs, our aching groans. He knows us far better than we know ourselves, knows our pregnant condition, and keeps us present before God. That's why we can be so sure that every detail in our lives of love for God is worked into something good."*
>
> — ROMANS 8:26-28, MSG

Activations For Learning to Be Loved

PERSISTENCE

Breath of life ~

"Keep on honey, keep going forward beloved, don't give up little one, one step at a time.

Take it one moment at a time, but DON'T GIVE UP! There's more going on than just this present moment – there is a whole new life being grown, deep within you and in the lives of others you may not even know but whose situations touch yours. ALL things, not just the little speck that you can see right now, are being worked into a beautiful whole, into new life, ready to be birthed, if only you will keep going."

Selah ~

Have you ever gotten stuck, unable to see a way through? Have you ever felt like you cannot go on one more second? What do you need to hang on for? Persist through?

Pray the Word ~

"Jesus, thank You that You never leave me, that You always have good plans for me, that when it seems like nothing good is happening, when I cannot see two steps in front of me, that there is always ONE step forward to take, even if it is simply to rest in You, or do the dishes... Thank You that You are building faith within. Thank You that I shall know You as never before as I keep going forward, persisting in trust for what I cannot yet see."

16

GRATITUDE

*H*arvard Medical School defines *gratitude* as "a thankful appreciation for what an individual receives, whether tangible or intangible."[1] I've had the privilege of good, mature-in-the-Kingdom-of-God friends who have exampled to me the value of being thankful and giving thanks, particularly in difficult situations. I've experienced the transforming power of it.

When we choose gratitude and persist in giving thanks, we become transformed! It is as rivers of Living Water washing through our being, breaking off chunks of bitterness and fear. Gratitude shifts our focus from inward to outward, self-pity to wonder, only seeing lack to seeing abundance all around—from death to life. Gratitude aligns us with God's perspective!

Gratitude says, "I trust You. I recognise your gifts. I trust that You love me, that You have purpose even in this, to help me know You better. To discover freedom."
Giving thanks, choosing Life, unveils a new way of seeing.

No Matter What

Even in Pip I've seen
Thanksgiving,
have seen her satisfied,
at peace;
Transformed by Trust,
needs met,
at Rest;
with expectation now
of being cared for:
she knows who we are,
that she can expect good from us.
No matter what.

Living with You for some time now
I've seen terrors and fears transformed
when I bring the sacrifice of Thanksgiving –
a Choice to give Thanks,
to be Grateful,
when I cannot See.
Because I have come to Know You –
that You are always Good.
No matter what.

Time and again
You've turned my focus
from what I Fear,
to see Your Face,
Your Eyes of Love, to hear
Your Heart of pure Promise,
to Truth:
I am Loved, Well,
hearing frequently:

Don't look at that –
Look at Me!

And now I don't even have to Choose,
I just Live there –
In Thanksgiving!
Everywhere I look,
You Are Present, Brilliant. Tender, Laughing!
Though sometimes hidden,
Seen and known with the eyes of my heart.

And I see and know More
than I ever did before –
and I am Overcome with Thanksgiving
heart welling and SWELLING
with GRATITUDE,
warm JOY,

No matter what!
You Redeem ALL.

Gratitude, in the end,
is the Purest expression of Praise,
confounding and crippling the enemy of our souls
who cannot understand,
in the midst of all our trials and his oppressions,
the Choice for Joy!

G.K. Chesterton once said, "I would maintain that thanks are the highest form of thought, and that gratitude is happiness doubled by wonder."[2]

In *The Artist's Way Everyday*, December 27, Julie Cameron penned:

> As a form of medicine for ourselves, we can consciously turn our thoughts to the ancient practice of practicing gratitude – a footfall at a time.
>
> Take yourself out-of-doors and set a goal of a simple twenty-minute walk. Aiming toward the outer world, allow your inner-world to fall into a brighter perspective by consciously —and concretely—enumerating your life's blessings.
>
> People, events, situations—any of these may be cause for gratitude. As you warm to your task of focusing on the good in your life, both your heart and your step will lighten.[3]

PIP?

Needy, an orphan, not knowing her worth,
her past not informing her future
Invitation from a heart
she doesn't yet trust
Trapped!
not knowing her freedom

Chosen for qualities she knows nothing of
Beautiful. unique, brilliant, fine
a mind of her own and a
clever observer
setting limits on what she'll accept

Wariness conflicted with longing
eager but ready to run
running but circling round back again
cautious but wants to jump in!

spunkily quiet
seriously playful
tentatively spontaneous
responsive yet cold
impatiently waiting but hating a push
fear seems a frequent companion

Slowly
softening
longer periods
of eyes closed serenely in rest
Small steps coming closer
more frequent connecting
less running away on her own
Nudging under the arm of relationship
less tentative
more frequently near

Features are softening
trust is developing
as she grows more comfortable with love... hmmm....

"Thank God no matter what happens."

— 1 THESSALONIANS 5:17, MSG

"Enter his gates with thanksgiving and his courts with praise, give thanks to him and praise his name. For the Lord is good and his love endures forever; his faithfulness continues through all generations."

— PSALM 100: 4-5, NIV

Activations For Learning to Be Loved

GRATITUDE

Selah ~

Is there anything going on in your life that's tough? that just will not budge or change?

Have you tried Gratitude? Persistently? Are you willing to begin now?

On That Note ~

The Breakthrough of Giving Thanks by Graham Cooke, the Faith Series.

Pray the Word ~

"Thank You for the reminder that when I choose thanksgiving, I begin to enter the courts of heaven, Your Throne Room, Your very Presence, and that changes everything!

Father, will You help me to more and more, in any situation but particularly those that are difficult, to respond quickly with thanks-

giving, with praise of You Who are good, Whose love endures forever, Your faithfulness surrounds me always. Will You build this gift, this trust response, deep within me? How I love You – thank You, my Father, for all Your love and faithfulness for me."

PART III

WORDS from SOUTH AFRICA, 2014

"Awake, awake, put on your strength, O Zion;
put on your beautiful garments,
O Jerusalem, the holy city;
for there shall no more come into you
the uncircumcised and the unclean.
Shake yourself from the dust and arise;
be seated, O Jerusalem;
loose the bonds from your neck,
O captive daughter of Zion."

Isaiah 52:1-2, ESV

Land of *More*

17

PENTECOST

On the Christian Church's Liturgical Year calendar, Pentecost is celebrated on the seventh Sunday after Easter, and is the celebration of the Holy Spirit of Living God being poured out in fullness upon 120 people: the early apostles and others as they were gathered in an upper room together praying, seeking God, seeking understanding, waiting as Jesus instructed following His death on the Cross and then His surprising appearing to them three days later – RESUR-RECTED, verified by hundreds of witnesses![1]

Holy Spirit was poured out upon these, appearing as tongues of fire, and as they went out amongst the people in this new fire from Heaven, they all spoke in languages previously unknown to them! Thousands heard and believed the good news of Jesus and miracles took place everywhere they went! It was the birth of the Church, and nothing was ever the same again![2] The wild-fire of the Living God spread across continents, changing lives of millions upon millions, bringing healing of hearts, minds, and bodies, impacting the arts, education, medical treatment, thought, ingenuity and more over the course of two hundred centuries.

Pentecost, June 4, 2014

During a service in a small denominational church the sermon, written by the pastor who was away and read by a layperson, claimed that the mighty works of the Holy Spirit detailed in the New Testament do not take place today, that all the "so-called revivals," testimonies of healings and miracles that have taken place over the years since then have been man-made, man-formed, man-worked up, and man-deceived.

And my spirit groaned loud within me, for I've met Him! Holy Spirit had been speaking to and acting through me (and many others) for years, and all around the world there are beyond multitudes of amazing documented testimonies of miraculous Presence, of healing and deliverance!

And I turned aside from this truly ignorant, empty-of-life shell of a "message of God," and I cried out silently within me, "O GOD, may I PLEASE go to South Africa?"

My husband Grant and I had been meeting with another church which was planning to take a small team to South Africa at the end of the summer. I'd never done anything like that before, for all kinds of fears and reasons.

And He said, "Yes."

> "Believe Me that I am in the Father and the Father is in Me; other-
> wise believe because of the works themselves. Truly, truly, I say to
> you, he who believes in Me, the works that I do, he will do also;
> and greater works than these he will do; because I go to the
> Father. Whatever you ask in My name, that will I do, so that the

Father may be glorified in the Son. If you ask Me anything in My name, I will do it.

If you love Me, you will keep My commandments.

I will ask the Father, and He will give you another Helper, that He may be with you forever; that is the Spirit of truth, whom the world cannot receive, because it does not see Him or know Him, but you know Him because He abides with you and will be in you."

— JOHN 14:11-17, NASB

Activations For Learning to Be Loved

PENTECOST

Selah ~

Have you ever had inklings or promptings – something long asleep beginning to stir you within to step out into unknown, into what previously would have been unthinkable for you, because you just KNOW in every cell that you MUST?

Has longing and leading ever overcome fear for you? Would you like it to?

Pray the Word ~

"Dear Jesus, I believe that the Father is in You and You are in the Father. I believe You have even greater works, miraculous works, works from Your heart of compassion for me to walk in, that You would be known. I love You, Jesus. I want to know You more, to obey You; I need Your Helper, Your Holy Spirit. I want to receive and live all You died and resurrected for me to receive and live, that Your Father, MY Father, may be glorified through YOU, through me.

Holy Spirit, I invite and receive You to live within and through me, to help me better know and glorify my Father."

18

COMPARE

*I*n August 2014, just a few months after my Pentecost heart cry, I travelled with a group from several churches in Canada, the United States, and Mossel Bay, South Africa. We brought an International Leader's School of Ministry (ILSOM) at the invitation of hungry-for-more people in Stellenbosch, South Africa. This was a time of great stretching and opportunity for me. I chose to present the teaching on *Ungodly Beliefs*. And though I have had no difficulty speaking to large groups of people in the past (having had lengthy experience in acting, presenting, singing, and leading), this presentation required preparation and releasing in a teaching capacity, and I am not a teacher—far from it, I am more of a "teller."

But God was doing a work in me.

Because access to the internet was very limited, I was cut off from communicating with husband Grant or friends back home. Holy Spirit and our team were truly the only ones I could communicate with and since the team members were all being hosted in different homes, there was often limited time even with each other! As well, the others on our team were long immersed in a different stream and expression of vital Christian faith that in many ways I had not been.

Although I had not experienced it fully myself, everything in me knew from the Scriptures that it was truth. My faith foundation was formed with an incredible group of God-lovers at a number of Lutheran churches and home fellowships. In addition, Grant and I had relationships with many from various denominations, receiving and loving the richness that each varied expression of God brought. With all this diversity, my foundation was rich in the Word (the Bible), in study and understanding, in the importance of community, in contemplation, in service to those in need, in prayer and intercessions, with a good beginning in the receiving and knowing of Holy Spirit and His gifts. However, my experience was not in the breadth, freedom, and expression of these that God had joined us with in this new season.

Even while knowing the validity of my own true and full experience with God, in South Africa I struggled with the question, did I have anything to offer compared with these from the CTF stream? I knew I was nothing like them! What to let go of? What to receive?

Did I have anything to give?

Compare[1] (verb)

- to be worthy of comparison (with)
- to be regarded as similar or equal
- to make comparisons
- to stand in comparison; measure up: how do I compare with...?

Comparing, comparing, comparing...feeling less-than, yet at the same time receiving all kinds of encouragement, affirmations, visions, discernment, and giftings to speak into the lives of those with whom we were gathered. It all actually converged well with the topic I'd be speaking on: a broken self-image birthed in untrue, false (ungodly) beliefs.... God had me right where He wanted me. He is always brilliant! and always drawing us further into MORE.

"For You formed my inward parts; You wove me in my mother's womb. I will give thanks to You, for I am fearfully and wonderfully made; Wonderful are Your works, And my soul knows it very well."

— PSALM 139:13-14, NASB

Activations For Learning to Be Loved

COMPARE

Selah ~

Have you ever recognised qualities in others that you were hungry for?

Have you compared yourself unfavourably, not recognising your own good giftings?

Have you recognised that coming alongside of these is an opportunity to learn and grow, to receive and also to quietly *be*, and to share what you've grown in as well?

Do you know your great strengths as well as your weaknesses?

Can you see our Father's wisdom and good design in needing each other to make a complete whole?

Pray the Word ~

"Father, forgive me for comparing myself to others. I am fearfully and wonderfully made! So are my sisters and brothers in You! You delight in each of us! You have given good gifts to me, created me just as You desire. Thank You. Help me to see myself through Your eyes, to

recognise Your good gifts in me, to see where I fit into Your Body, what I have to offer to the whole. Help me too, to graciously recognise and receive what others in the Body bring as well – no competition, simply a full representation of Jesus."

19

LISTEN

*S*ince Jesus came to me visually in Spirit and felt Presence in 1980, I have conversed long and life-givingly well with Him, filling many journals with my questions, prayers and conversations (writing helps me focus), and with His constant giving of illumination, direction, encouragement, revelation and peace.

Listen[1] (verb)

• To give attention to someone or something in order to hear him, her, or it.

One of the main foundational teachings in an International Leaders School of Ministry is "Hearing God's Voice" – revolutionary learning for anyone who has not experienced this before! It is based on teaching from Dr. Mark Virkler, who was inspired by Holy Spirit through Habakkuk 2:1-2 as he sought how to hear God, knowing that Jesus had said that His sheep hear His voice and follow Him.[2]

"I will stand on my guard post And station myself on the rampart; And I will watch to see what He will speak to me, And how I may reply when I am reproved.

Then the Lord answered me and said, "Record the vision And inscribe it on tablets, That the one who reads it may run. For the vision is yet for the appointed time; It hastens toward the goal and it will not fail. Though it tarries, wait for it; For it will certainly come, it will not delay."

— HABAKKUK 2:1-3, NASB

As exemplified in Habakkuk 2:1-3, there are four keys to hearing God's voice:

1. I will stand on my guard post (be still).
2. I will keep watch to see (fix your eyes on Jesus).
3. He will speak to me (tune to spontaneity).
4. Then the Lord answered me and said, "Record the vision." (Write the flow of thoughts and pictures that light upon your heart and mind.)[3]

In addition to further teaching on this, there is an exercise after the teaching which gives opportunity – the first time for many – to hear God speak. This exercise always brings new responses from Holy Spirit depending on what is on God's heart to speak and reveal.

On this particular day in South Africa, we were encouraged to ask Father the fun question, "What game do You want to play with me?"

I heard, "Ballroom dancing!"

"Why do You want to do this with me?" I asked.

"Because I want to take you in My arms and lead you, flying across the dance floor. I love you, and I want to lead you in My arms, to hold you and help you fly!"

With the eyes of my heart I saw Jesus swirling me around grandly, lifting my feet off the floor, my full skirt whirling and twirling, round and round and round, our faces full of laughter and joy!

He was leading; all I had to do was follow. No effort at all.

Another question was: "Lord, if there's any place in the world where You would like to meet with me, where would it be? Why? What do You want to tell me?"

He responded, "Here in South Africa, because you are free from many other responsibilities and supports, and I can lead you out on a limb, and be your only safety. You are being taken beyond your limits, and it is safe. I will not shame or disappoint you."

Another day during this time I asked, "What do you have for me, what do You want to say to me today?"

"Why don't you just climb up on My Father's knee and be held?" And my Daddy said (as I leaned against Him, feeling small, vulnerable, and a little weepy):

> "That little girl within need not hide and remain alone any longer. That little girl need not be silent anymore. That little girl may come out now and grow into her womanhood – at rest, unafraid. I have put My words in your mouth and covered you with the shadow of My hand. I will give you voice.
> As I told Moses, I tell you, do not be in fear or dread of anyone or any situation, for I AM, and I go before you to prepare your way. I will give you all you need.

Remember all you have been learning, not the least of
which is to NOT speak if you do not hear Me speaking,
and do not 'add to' when you do hear Me speak.
Simply be. Simply be.
You have become and are becoming a woman of rest. A
woman who can be trusted. A woman who will minister
My heart.
Do not fill in empty spaces. Let them be."

My heart responded, "Thank You my Father. Your strong arms
hold me. You do not send me far away from You but give Jesus
to walk alongside, within, Your Spirit's presence to rest and
speak, encourage, love. Thank You Jesus for Your extreme love!
Hide me in Your embrace. Keep me in the secret place with
You. Keep me and remind me to not compare myself with any
of Your other kids. Your word and Your call to me are personal
and particular and Good! I want all You have and want to give
me! Take me up the stairway to the heavenly places, soak me,
saturate me in Your presence this day."

> *"Lovers of God have been given eyes to see with spiritual discern-
> ment and ears to hear from God."*
>
> — PROVERBS 20:12, TPT

Activations For Learning to Be Loved

LISTEN

Breath of Life ~

"Safety beloved, no Fear
Though you dwell in the midst of trouble, have no fear.
I AM with you, to protect you.
I go before you to prepare your way – which is My way.
I go behind you to protect you.
I go beneath you to be your Rock, your Foundation,
your Support.
I walk beside you as your Friend, your Bridegroom, your
Confidant, your Teacher.
I walk within you as your Rest and
I AM above you to be your Glory and the lifter of your
head.
No fear – in anything – for you know that perfect love
casts out fear and I love you perfectly! Be still. Know
Me. Rest."

Selah ~

Right now: quiet yourself down, focus on Jesus, ask what game your Father wants to play with you, and why? Become aware of that still, small voice, and write down what you see and hear.

Be Loved.

On That Note ~

One Thing Remains by Jesus Culture

Pray the Word ~

"God, I love you. I long to hear Your voice. You are the giver of seeing eyes, hearing ears. Thank You that You desire to speak with me as much as I long to hear You! Please give me the spiritual discernment to know and hear how and when You are speaking."

20

MORE

J was staying at a home which was located on the boundary of a large animal park outside Stellenbosch, South Africa. As I was seated on a balcony, an ostrich was running freely by, a donkey brayed in a pen off to the left, lions roared in the distance, and burglar bars on the windows and locked gate kept intruders out.

I was preparing the teaching on Ungodly Beliefs that I would present the next day.

As I quieted my heart, I heard:

"Awake Janis Awake!
Put on your strength!
Clothe yourself in robes of splendour!
You carry My rest.
I AM raising you up, up to new heights; only keep in Me.
You shall be in My throne room always. You shall carry My presence, My quiet, My glory, out into the fray of

lives. You shall do it all as you dwell in Me, in our secret abiding place.

Continue to seek Me, continue to hunger after Me, and I shall give you more.

You shall know Me more, as you seek Me.

I shall take you into many places and situations – I AM your safety.

I AM your shelter and your refuge and your strength.

I AM shall never fail you – never!

There is always more!! More than you know or expect or imagine!

I will take you to the nations,

I will take you far,

I will take you wide.

I have put My word in your mouth and hide you in the shadow of My hand because you love Me, you know and understand My Name, your heart is for Me, your eyes are on Me, therefore you are safe – safe to carry My presence, safe to carry My power, safe to speak and touch with My freedom.

You have cultivated a quiet heart and your soul truly is a baby content.[1]

You minister My quiet –

I AM well pleased My daughter, My flying one, My beauty – you are learning to have no regard for any one, any man's regard, only for Mine, therefore, I can take you far. Rest in Me."

More[2] (adjective)

- In greater quantity, amount, measure, degree, or number:
- Additional or further.

In South Africa, my Father gave me many, many instances of His particular knowing and loving – just for little me, all by my timid self. He kept giving and promising more: arranging that I would be hosted beside a lion park. (I love lions!)

Remember my sense of inadequacy I spoke of earlier? I was loved, appreciated, and honoured by my host during the first portion of the journey, Labare and her soon-to-be fiancé Gileam, as well as the wonderful people who came to the ILSOM week. I felt treated and honoured like a queen. Later in the trip I was given the most beautiful room with what even looked to be a throne in the amazing Perseverantia Exclusive Guesthouse (Perseverance—remember that?) on Gordon's Baai. "You are Royalty!" Holy Spirit whispered.

Here, Holy Spirit affirmed even more quietly His love, His always-presence, and His continuing whispered invitation to stillness. Early one morning, a wee brown bird came with little bits of grass and twig to build a small nest in the awning above my head...and sat on my railing, looking at me, lingering long (when I was still and quiet enough). I saw and heard the call to stillness once more—what it looked like and what it felt like.

> "Never doubt God's mighty power to work in you and accomplish all this. He will achieve INFINITELY MORE than your greatest request, your most unbelievable dream, and exceed your wildest imagination! He will outdo them all, for his miraculous power constantly energizes you."

> — EPHESIANS 3:20, TPT, EMPHASIS ADDED

Activations For Learning to Be Loved

MORE

Selah ~

Are you hearing, do you KNOW, that all God's whispers to me are for you too? Are you hungry for His MORE? Is your heart's cry to know Him, to understand His Name? If so, what could your MORE look like?

What are your heart longings for? can you hear His Whisper?

Have you seen /heard the beginnings? Are you ready to be surprised?

Pray the Word ~

"God, You are amazing! I have trouble even fathoming that You could have MORE for me than I can imagine in my wildest dreams... Enlarge my vision, my trust, my rest in You, that I may see, hear, receive all You want to give to me, all You want to do through me."

21

JOURNEY

I am not typically a dreamer, but some weeks after returning home from South Africa, I had a dream in which I was preparing to go on quite a journey, to a place I'd never been before.

Journey [1] (noun)

- A traveling from one place to another, usually taking a rather long time.
- A distance, course, or area traveled or suitable for traveling.
- A period of travel.
- Passage or progress from one stage to another.

In the dream, before beginning the journey, a small brown bird, very much like the little brown bird on my balcony in Gordon's Baai, South Africa, came and sat on my shoulder, staying there throughout the entire journey. I was in complete quietness of spirit, restful, and in the dream, I met many others along the way who were helpful, warm, friends. I recognised many of them as being from our new CTF Calgary family.

And I heard God say:

"I am taking you on a journey. I will be with you constantly and will be your Peace. I will bring many safe people alongside to journey with you. And you will reach your destination well."

(Weeks later, very weary from needs of others and my own self, He spoke further.)

"... the Word I gave P for you regarding swimming deeper and deeper, going further and further into the depths of intimacy with Me and being raised up to the high heights of the eagle, to soar and fly above – I gave you that for good reason.

Sit with it. Live in it. Receive it. Lower to go higher. Humility goes before honour.
You are My cherished beloved; I will heal your orphan tendencies – that place that still longs for and needs affirmation. Remember the gift of South Africa – that was My heart for you – loved, valued, met, understood: encouragement, affirmation, recognition and reception, healing, joy in you and through you, anointing – Never forget what was sown into you there – all My love for you, My princess, My Bride.

I AM weaning you from needing the affirmation and recognition of man. Only seek Me, only seek to love Me, to hear My voice, to follow My lead. I call you to humility, to quiet, to seeing with My eyes and serving as I reveal need. I lead you in it all, that My rest and My joy will be as natural to you as fresh springs bubbling over, in brightness and refreshing clarity, pure, easy, no silt, no question, only bubbling over in joy, and freedom. Lower, quieter, to My depths, and you shall fly.

Love Me. Love Me. Love Me, and My love will fill you to such an extent that you will indeed have new weighty love for the masses, all those who are lost, wounded, needing to be carried, encouraged.
My gift through you will be joy!"

A confirmation of this word came to my email inbox just days later in the form of a teaching from Derek Prince Ministries on the very same theme: "The Way Up is Down."

Thus began the next leg of the journey: lower to go higher, with what turned out to be wracking tears to discover Joy...healing from the inside out.

Faith motivated Abraham to obey God's call and leave the familiar to discover the territory he was destined to inherit from God. So he left with only a promise and without even knowing ahead of time where he was going, Abraham stepped out in faith.

— HEBREWS 11:8, TPT

<u>Activations For Learning to Be Loved</u>

JOURNEY

Selah ~

What might your new journey with God encompass?

What may you need to leave behind in order to go forward?

What are the feelings, thoughts that rise up? How do you respond to: 'The Way Up is Down'? Are you willing?

Pray the Word ~

"God, I want faith like Abraham's – hearing Your leading, willing to begin to step out in faith and trust that You will lead each moment, without me even knowing where I am going. I remember that Abraham had a LOT of challenges along that lengthy journey and made a LOT of mistakes, but he grew more and more fully into a righteous man, known to all that came after him as one who lived by faith. May I hear the promises You have for me to stand on, courage and trust to leave what is known, that I may discover the territory You are calling to, grow into maturity, and receive my full inheritance of all You have for me."

"I formed your inward parts;
I knit you together in your mother's womb.
Do not fear, for I have redeemed you; I have called you by
name; you are Mine!"

from Psalm 139:13 and Isaiah 43:1, ESV

―――――――

"For there is nothing hidden that shall not be
disclosed, nor anything secret that shall not be known and
come out into the open."

Luke 8:17, AMPC

22

IDENTITY

*T*he cry of every awakening heart is, "Who am I? Who and what am I made for? Do I have any value? What is my purpose?" And, because we live in a broken world that is actually a battleground to keep us from knowing our worth and identity in Jesus (what our reason for being is), we frequently have not heard God's heart for us. Instead, we hear and believe things that aren't true: failure, stupid, weak, useless and so on.

Throughout my time in South Africa and in the weeks and months following, Abba affirmed my identity: who He had designed me to be. Through varieties of people and situations, He spoke some words I had heard before (Daughter, Bride) but which had not greatly affected me. I hadn't heard with my "heart ears" so I wasn't impacted with the magnitude of these words. Some I was angry with, even offended by for a while because I did not see the fullness from His perspective (a casserole?? yuck!).

It came to me many months later that this affirming of identity was an important preparation for the journey Abba Father had earlier said He would be taking me on.

A solid foundation of faith and relationship with Him was built so that I would know the rock-solidness of His Word and character and purposes, and that, regardless of appearances, He is utterly faithful; He could be trusted. And He would not leave me where I was, with what had often overtaken me many times in my life, often showing up unexpectedly: a seemingly bottomless, unstoppable, unexplainable well of tears.

I came to recognise that Abba had brought me to a people, a place, and a time when He was preparing me for deep heart surgery. The gift of learning to hear His voice more clearly, hearing His encouragements and loving affirmations of who I'd been created to be, having experience of His playfulness and safety, all gave me a safe place to BE.

My own Words of Identity and Promise:

- **Bride of the King:** Cherished, desired, delighted in, gifted, anointed, with authority; Royalty!

- **Carrier** (of my Father's heart): A carrier is a person or thing that carries, holds, or conveys something.[1]

- **Casserole(!):** A dish in which food may be baked and served. A stew or side dish cooked and served in a casserole.[2] But noted for me: not a bland inexpensive casserole made of leftovers thrown together and thus nothing special (my first thoughts on hearing *casserole*), not defined by one gift or ability (flavour!), but rather full of many enticing flavours and gifts.

- **Daughter** (of God) – A girl or woman in relation to her parents.[3] In loving Jesus I too become a loved and provided-for child of God![4]

- **Fearfully and Wonderfully Made:** Awesomely created! Even the revelation of Myers Briggs Defender/Sentinel spoke life and encouragement. Characteristics I thought were flaws requiring effort to correct are actually part of God's unique creating, knitting together in Mom's womb – gifts, not mistakes; needing wisdom and balance, but celebrating too!

- **Iron Fist in a Velvet Glove:** Used to describe someone who seems to be gentle but is in fact forceful and determined (I've got a Fire in my bones!). "Great compassion, severe strength," Holy Spirit whispered.

- **Resplendent** –The adjective resplendent comes from a Latin word that means *to shine brightly*; attractive and impressive through being richly colourful or sumptuous! Synonyms include brilliant, dazzling, glittering. Look up Resplendent Quetzal and see colourful!!!

- **Safe** (for others to be with): Protected from or not exposed to harm, danger or risk.

All these and more were spoken as my identity, drawing me into a place of quiet and trust as He brought me forward, preparing me to go through something that would require believing to my very core that I was loved.

And that He had life on the other side of it.

> *"...the one who prophesies (speaks what God speaks) speaks to people for edification [to promote their spiritual growth] and [speaks words of] encouragement [to uphold and advise them concerning the matters of God] and [speaks words of] consolation [to compassionately comfort them]."*

— 1 CORINTHIANS 14:3, AMP

> *"...body and soul, I am marvelously made..."*

— PSALM 139:14, MSG

> *"But now, thus says the Lord, your Creator, O Jacob, And He who formed you, O Israel, "Do not fear, for I have redeemed you; **I have called you by name; you are Mine!**"*

— ISAIAH 43:1, NASB, EMPHASIS ADDED

Activations For Learning to Be Loved

IDENTITY

Selah ~

Do you have people in your life who will listen to the heart of God for you, who speak truth and life, who see what God sees when He looks at you, who get excited about what He is doing and leading to, no matter what is going on in in the natural at the moment? Have you stopped to ask and listen for yourself?

Pray the Word ~

"Lord God, Father, Friend – Thank You that You know me, You know my name, You know who You made me to be. Once again, I ask to always hear and live from Who You say I am. When I cannot hear for myself, will You bring others who listen well, to encourage me to see my identity in You. Help me to know it is not conceit or pride that drives this request, it is all about fact and truth, receiving a solid foundation, celebrating Your goodness!"

23

HELP

*E*vents began taking place, incidents, emotions, reactions: fear, FEAR! anger, ANGER! swirling CONFUSION! yet I heard the call to trust all the way, with quiet leading underneath (which I recognised even in the midst of the noise), no pressure, no pushing, but instead the quiet promise of Presence. Safety.

Help[1] (verb)

- To give or provide what is necessary to accomplish a task or satisfy a need; contribute strength or means to; render assistance to; cooperate effectively with; aid; assist.
- To save; rescue; succor.
- To make easier or less difficult; contribute to; facilitate.

I felt completely incapable of sorting through all the thoughts and emotions that kept rising up. I knew I needed help and chose to meet with a counsellor I trusted who was safe, who was trained, who would listen for God's heart and help me find my way through.

> *"The Lord is my strength and my shield; My heart trusts in him, and I am helped."*
>
> — PSALM 28:7, NIV

> *"And I am convinced and sure of this very thing, that He Who began a good work in you will continue until the day of Jesus Christ (right up to the time of His return), developing (that good work) and perfecting and bringing it to full completion in you."*
>
> — PHILIPPIANS 1:6, AMPC

> *Don't panic. I'm with you. There's no need to fear for I'm your God. I'll give you strength. I'll help you. I'll hold you steady, keep a firm grip on you.*
>
> — ISAIAH 41:10, MSG

Activations For Learning to Be Loved

HELP

Breath of Life ~

"Do not be afraid, I AM with you. I go before you to prepare the way. I have never left you. Though man has corrupted My desire for good for you, I have been with you and shielded and been refuge and protector though you have not known it.

You are precious to Me – you are delicate and fine. I have not sought to dishonour you, to be confusing to you, to withhold anything from you. I have sought to lead you into rest, into preparing you to hear and receive in this next season, that it would not overwhelm you. You have needed to begin to know what it is to dwell in My secret place of rest and safety. You have needed to know and experience the True. It has been My gentleness for you, that you would know My safety, that you would know I AM with you and will never shame or offend you. You can trust Me to lead you well into healing, into freedom, into life, into calling."

Selah ~

Have you ever come to a time when you knew you could not make your way through alone? When all was confusion? When the situation was beyond praying, asking, or waiting? When you needed help? Are you there now?

Pray the Word ~

"Father, I am so thankful that just as You promised Your people long ago, You promise me that You are my Helper, that I need not ever fear. Thank You for Your promise that You are always taking me forward, that You WILL complete the good work You've begun in me, completing in experience the wholeness, health, and life, that Jesus won for me. Please guide me in not just talking wildly to anyone, everyone, about the need I am in. Do You have someone who is safe, who will listen with me for Your heart, give guidance and Your good counsel to help untangle what I cannot yet see through?"

24

TAKE MY HAND

a few days after meeting with my counselor, during a time of music and worshiping God in community at church, feeling confused with a multitude of thoughts, Jesus appeared in front of me and reached His hand out toward me.

I reached out my hand and took His.

His hand was large, warm, slightly calloused to the touch...and I knew I could trust Him to take me through whatever was coming.

I was in Peace.

And I was ready to go deeper with my counselor, to uncover what was hidden, what was causing so much pain.

"O God, you are my God; I earnestly search for you. My soul thirsts for you; my whole body longs for you in this parched and weary land where there is no water. I have seen you in your sanctuary and gazed upon your power and glory. Your unfailing love is better than life itself; how I praise you! I will praise you as long as I live, lifting up my hands to you in prayer. You satisfy me more

than the richest feast. I will praise you with songs of joy. I lie awake thinking of you, meditating on you through the night. Because you are my helper, I sing for joy in the shadow of your wings. I cling to you; your strong right hand holds me securely."

— PSALM 63:1-8, NLT

"When you pass through the waters, I will be with you, and through the rivers, they will not overwhelm you. When you walk through the fire, you will not be burned or scorched, nor will the flame kindle upon you."

— ISAIAH 43:2, AMPC

Activations For Learning to Be Loved

TAKE MY HAND

Breath of Life ~

"My precious child – no fear, NO need to fear, I AM
here, I will go ahead of you and prepare the good way.
Take care to keep your mind free of imagining possibilities – simply give yourself over into My care and I will
carry you. Take hold of My Son's hand, feel and know
His presence, His safety, His goodness – for He – My
beloved Son – is My image – He carries all My heart for
you.

Though you will be led on a path you do not know, He
will be gentle for you but also a Mighty Protector. You
are right in knowing and anticipating My coming JOY to
you, and to your household, and the coming enlarging
of your tent.
You have learned to dwell and abide and rest in My
secret place, where I commune with you. You have
learned to hear and know My voice.
I will make the way clear. I will lead through to the
other side.

The time will not be fruitless, rather it will be freeing, and you will know My profound peace, and be filled with My overflowing overabundant waves of exultant JOY.

Do not fear. Take My hand and move forward."

On That Note ~

Oceans (Where Feet May Fail) by Hillsong UNITED. Songwriters Joel Houston, Matt Crocker/Solomon Lighthelm

---

Selah ~

Are you willing to take Jesus' hand, go where He leads, even if it's scary? Can you choose to trust His Promise, even through tears, that He HAS and WILL complete His GOOD purposes for YOU? That He HAS Good purposes for you? That He brings EVERYTHING together into a Good you cannot even see or imagine right now? That His scope is W I D E R than just you?

Pray the Word ~

"Jesus, thank You for Your promise to be with me when I am faced with challenging things, that You will take me through them safely, that You are my covering, my protector, my strong shield. Keep my eyes on You, constantly looking to You."

Activate the Word ~

Take some time and meditate on the words of Psalm 63:1-8.
Read them out loud, talk to God about them, let them infuse
your being; perhaps make them your own prayer, and your
thanksgiving.

25

REVELATION, LOSS, AND
RESURRECTION

*O*ver quite a number of years, pictures had occasionally flashed in my mind's eye. With the gifted non-manipulative help of clinical counsellor Darrin Derksen of Live2b-Free, over the course of several visits I was able to recognise more fully what had taken place when I was around four years of age. The revelation of that included not only seeing events, but also growing revelation of all that had been lost in my life from that time forward.

Pondering and praying following one of these visits, I saw that Jesus was right there at the time, and that He took the offense upon Himself. It was a profound revelation that effectively gave me a new beginning – a resurrection – to be worked out over a period of time: retroactively in spirit, presently in each day, and going forward for every day in the future. I received much grace to forgive the offender completely – a very necessary aspect of healing, releasing not only myself but the other as well from the chains that held and affected us both, even these many years later.

Revelation[1]

- (verb) The act of revealing or disclosing; disclosure.
- (noun) Something revealed or disclosed, especially a striking disclosure, as of something not before realized.

Loss[2] (noun)

- Detriment, disadvantage, or deprivation from failure to keep, have, or get;
- The state or feeling of grief when deprived of someone or something of value;
- Having something or someone leave or be taken away from you;
- Feeling of grief when something is gone.

Resurrect[3] (verb)

- To bring someone back to life:
- To bring back something into use or existence that had disappeared or ended.

ON LOSS OF LIFE & RESURRECTION

A spunky sparkly little girl went in
A flattened empty shell came out

Innocence and Life met Confusion and Death
IMPOSED SILENCE
lost voice
paralysis

FEAR overshadowing everything from then on
walls thick high
keeping separate, unseen
hidden well
perfectly masked

quiet responses, don't make waves
hard to breathe
stillness
(silencing the roar)

flickers of heart (Your warm breath?) connecting,
    responding
always for underdog, recognising value
small attempts to find way
sometimes defiant
effort, so much effort
crumbling over and over
into emptiness
only a spectator to others' successes
always on the outside
looking on

But formed into a Seer

You carried that flattened empty shell of a spunky
    sparkly girl out in Your arms
Holy You took in Yourself the desecration she received
    even as she lived it
You held her close to Your breast
You wept over her and hid her too –

Within Your heart.

two kinds of hiddenness
one death, one life
both unseen
until....

not a sudden Resurrection
but a safe and gentle journey
begun and maintained in Your quiet
as You loved
turned on the Lights!
revealed YourSELF
and held out Your hand

Come up here:
Here I AM

A new journey beginning
with balm of Healing, road markers of Hope
of Presence
 of Truth: My Faithfulness Surrounds You, I will
     Never Leave You;
of Promise: I will never shame you. I will restore all
     that has been stolen
glimmers
sometimes great Fountains
of JOY!
first layer coming Alive to Love
empty shell beginning Resuscitation

There's been
many

more

layers

And now we're deep.

And that flattened empty shell
is regaining her Voice.

Here I am.

"The thief comes only in order to steal and kill and destroy. I came
that they may have and enjoy life, and have it in abundance (to the
full, til it overflows)!"

— JOHN 10:10, AMPC

"[She said] I am only a little rose or autumn crocus of the plain of
Sharon, or a [humble] lily of the valleys [that grows in deep and
difficult places]. But Solomon replied, Like the lily among thorns, so
are you, my love, among the daughters.

He brought me to the banqueting house, and his banner over me
was love [for love waved as a protecting and comforting banner
over my head when I was near him].

My beloved speaks and says to me, Rise up, my love, my fair one,
and come away. For, behold, the winter is past; the rain is over and
gone, the flowers appear on the earth; the time of the singing [of
birds] has come, and the voice of the turtledove is heard in our land.

The fig tree puts forth and ripens her green figs, and the vines are in
blossom and give forth their fragrance.

Arise, my love, my fair one, and come away.

So I went with him, and when we were climbing the rocky steps up the hillside, my beloved shepherd said to me] O my dove, [while you are here] in the seclusion of the clefts in the solid rock, in the sheltered and secret place of the cliff, let me see your face, let me hear your voice; for your voice is sweet, and your face is lovely."

— SONG OF SOLOMON 2:1, 4, 10-14, AMPC

Activations For Learning to Be Loved

REVELATION, LOSS, AND RESURRECTION

Selah ~

Have you ever experienced, coming closer and closer to the surface, revealing of trauma? This may be an event or a series of events, a moment in time or a long-drawn-out-seeming-forever, that shocked and traumatised you to the core. Have you known things were stolen from you? And have you experienced a coming awareness that Jesus restores?

Pray the Word ~

"Jesus, thank You that You have been with me on every rocky difficult path; thank You that You invite me to meet You there, that You hide me there, love me; You love my face, the sound of my voice. Thank You that though there is a very real thief that tries everything in his power to steal, kill and destroy all of life and joy, that You have come to bring life and redemption of every stolen moment. You are life and You redeem all beyond what I can imagine."

26

CALLING

One definition of "calling" from Merriam-Webster is "a strong inner impulse toward a particular course of action, especially when accompanied by conviction of divine influence."[1] Collins Dictionary defines it this way:

> "A calling is a profession or which someone is strongly attracted to, one which involves other people."[2]

Several weeks after the full revelation of that first offense, I talked with my Father:

Journal Entry - January 2015

> "Though I've chosen forgiveness, my heart still has a sense of being wounded, knocked back. Father – here I am with You. Thank You for Your quiet presence. Wash me with Jesus' sacrificial, victorious blood, fill me with Your Spirit.

Thank You that You bring all things together for good – You are always good! All Your paths are full of Your steadfast, full, perfect love and faithfulness!![3]

My Papa, my Abba – I feel wounded and still in need of Your healing touch. I resist going to [counsellor] DD again (because of distance, cost, a feeling it is something that would be ongoing forever, and frustration/unbelief/irritability re the 'process') – but which I recognise HAS been effectual in the past – so this response is negative/reactionary and something that I think is keeping me from getting help and further insight …

Jesus – will You let me just sit, BE with You today? Help me hear my Father's voice, know His heart. Because all I really want today is to be alone – with You – to cry, to listen, to allow expression. And I so look forward to CTF tonight – I look forward to being in Your Presence corporately – I am hungry for experience of You, Your manifest felt Presence.

O come; O come – thank You that You ARE here – You are Emmanuel – God with us.

Cleanse, deliver me from all that keeps me from seeing, hearing You.

O would You hold Your little vulnerable lily, Your little crocus, Your rose – fill me with Your strength – Your Fire – Your seeing, Your fragrance, Your determination to see Your kingdom in the lives of those held in bondage.

Wash over me Spirit of God.

Wash through me.

Pour into me the Living Waters from the throne of heaven,

Replenish me,

Deliver me from all the unbelief and despair.

I want to be one of Your burning ones –

Full of Your Life,

Full of Your HOPE.

Full of Your Joy.

Show me how all these qualities 'fit', express in/through PEACE. Through REST.

O Come O Come Emmanuel!"

In response, I heard these whispered words from Isaiah 61:1-3:

"The Spirit of the LORD is upon me because the LORD has anointed me to preach good news to the poor – He has sent me to bind up the brokenhearted, to proclaim freedom to the captives and release from darkness for the prisoners, to proclaim the year of the LORD's favour and the day of vengeance of our God, to comfort all who mourn, and provide for those who grieve in Zion – to bestow on them a crown of beauty instead of ashes, the oil of gladness instead of mourning, and a garment of praise instead of a spirit of despair." (AMPC)

In Luke 4, it is recounted that Jesus read the above passage, sat down, and said that that very day, this Scripture, written over 700 years before He was born, was fulfilled in Him.

Holy Spirit continued speaking to me:

"...rebuild the ancient ruins, restore the places long devastated, renew the ruined cities that have been devastated for generations ...

and you will be called the <u>priests of the LORD</u>, you will be named <u>ministers of our God</u> ... instead of their shame, my people will receive a double portion, and instead of disgrace they will rejoice in their inheritance; ... and so they will inherit a DOUBLE PORTION, in their land, and everlasting joy shall be theirs. For I the LORD love JUSTICE..." Isaiah 61:4-8 (AMPC, emphasis mine).

"I call you to restore JUSTICE, bringing the victory of Jesus' death and resurrection into the lives of those long devastated, even for generations; to bring My Son's victory into their wounds and brokenness and deliver into My Kingdom JOY."

I responded, "How??!! I have no training, no ability, and I always feel so ill-equipped!! Also, what do my tears and pain in the place of unfulfilled creative expression have to do with this?"

To which He lovingly replied:

> "Testimony. I will bring testimony of deliverance and healing. Watch and see. I say to you, let yourself fall back into My arms and let Me carry you. You have been oppressed and afflicted and I AM preparing your deliverance.
>
> These feelings of upheaval and upset are only the coming closer to the surface of that which I will deliver you from. Do not fear, neither be discouraged nor dismayed. I AM with you."

Activations For Learning to Be Loved

CALLING

Selah ~

Are you stuck in the Revealing or in the Loss? Have you begun to move into Resurrection? Have you heard a whisper of a calling – His transforming of curse into blessing, of death into Life? Can you still hope and believe, that Resurrection is coming, even if you don't see what it looks like yet? And that it may lead into your whole purpose for Being?

Are you willing for the journey?

On That Note ~

Captured (album) by Roberto and Kimberley Rivera

Pray the Word ~

"Holy Father, dear Jesus – Help me to hear and see some of what You are leading to on the other side of pain. Your redeeming Spirit sets

captives free, opens blind eyes, and turns death into beautiful life. Help me to lay back into Your strong arms and trust You to carry me. Thank You that Your faithfulness surrounds me, and You will not leave me in this stuck place but will take me THROUGH it to the place of Your destiny and purpose for me."

— PART V —

WORDS of EXPLANATION

*"For the Lord gives wisdom; from his mouth
come knowledge and understanding."*

Proverbs 2:6, ESV

27

FREEDOM FROM FEAR

*A*fter revelation of deep, early trauma comes further revelation and understanding of how it has impacted your whole identity and being throughout the years that follow, the result of responding to all of life from that bent and broken place.

Holy Spirit whispered:

"You've been entrenched upon – forced into a mold not of your or My making. It has not allowed you to grow and flourish as I intended for you."

Entrenched

When you're *entrenched*, you're dug in. Sometimes that means you're literally in a trench, but usually it means you just won't budge from a position or belief. Entrenched things are buried so solidly that they can't move — or just behave like they're firmly lodged in some deep hole.[1]

These definitions witnessed deeply within me. I remembered several portrayals I'd drawn years earlier to capture my feelings: drawings of being chained to concrete; of being in a deep hole with no way out; of being led in chains by a dark figure; of tears raining down from hands praying at the Cross; of two lookalike mirror-image girls (I knew they were young me) peeking out from behind opposite walls, crying, afraid to come out and be seen.

Sublimation

One day, I heard the word "sublimation."

Sublimation is one way that the ego reduces the anxiety that can be created by unacceptable urges or feelings. Sublimation works by channeling negative and unacceptable impulses into behaviors that are positive and socially acceptable.[2]

Reading this definition, I pondered which "socially acceptable actions or behavior" my young self had sublimated. In place of "socially unacceptable impulses" such as exposing wounded areas, expressing my opinion, bringing disturbance, accusing, letting my own need be known, or saying "No," I recognised life-long choosing of quiet, of smiling, not making waves, and people pleasing to the extreme. I also understood the "why" behind my failure to thrive or complete all the projects or activities in which I had attempted to involve myself over the years. University, theatre classes, art classes, various programs of study, various vocations that I considered: each one strongly piqued my interest for a time but then faded. Even my attempts in creativity were frequently full of taut tension within, and most always ended in tears.

Not so much sublimation, but a sense of being submerged, held down, as a weight on my very chest, making it difficult to move or breathe, my direction lost...

Fear

Fear is "an unpleasant, distressing emotion or thought that you have when you are frightened or worried by something danger-ous, painful, or bad that is happening or might happen."[3]

Fear, when there is good reason, is a warning to take action to protect yourself. When there is no true substantial reason present, fear is irrational, oppressive, and can be completely overpowering. Under the influence of fear, you may feel that very few people can be trusted and that nowhere and/or nothing is safe. I remember that the biggest reason I loved and married my husband Grant was that he was safe, and he made me feel safe (although I didn't recognise that reason at the time, only in hindsight).

Irrational fear must be the most common tactic of the enemy of our souls because in the Bible God instructs us to "Fear not, do not be afraid, have no anxiety" 365 times – one verse for every single day of the year!

Isaiah prophesied that the coming Messiah would be the Prince of Peace:

> *"For a child will be born to us, a son will be given to us; And the government will rest on His shoulders; And His name will be called Wonderful   Counselor,   Mighty   God,   Eternal Father, Prince of Peace."*
>
> — ISAIAH 9:6, NASB

"Peace I leave with you; My [own] peace I now give and bequeath to you. Not as the world gives do I give to you. Do not let your hearts be troubled, neither let them be afraid. [Stop allowing yourselves to be agitated and disturbed; and do not permit yourselves to be fearful and intimidated and cowardly and unsettled.]"

— JOHN 14:27, AMPC

Philippians 4:6-7 never fails to encourage me:

"Do not be anxious about anything, but in every situation, by prayer and petition, with thanksgiving, present your requests to God. And the peace of God, which transcends all understanding, will guard your hearts and your minds in Christ Jesus."

— PHILIPPIANS 4:6-7, NIV

"There is no fear in love, but perfect love casts out fear."

— 1 JOHN 4:18, ESV

These verses frequently washed over my being, Jesus settling deep within...until I became Peace...and Fearless.

Activations For Learning to Be Loved

FREEDOM FROM FEAR

Selah ~

Have you ever felt deeply entrenched in a place from which you cannot escape, chained to something so solid, what, you do not even know? Sublimated to the almost complete extinction of your personality – you do not even know who you are? Submerged so that you cannot breathe? Have you taken on any "socially acceptable" responses to life to protect your inner self? Have you lived with almost constant fear?

On that Note ~

No Longer Slaves by Jonathan and Melissa Helser/Bethel Music

Pray the Word ~

"O Jesus – How I need You. You ARE Peace, and Peace is what You bring always, whenever I turn to You. Thank You that it is Your desire and plan that I shall come to know the fullness of Your love, that Your love delivers me from all fear. Help me to know and experi-

ence that deliverance in every cell of my being. I give You all my fear, all within that I do not understand as yet, and receive Your Peace once more."

Activate the Word ~

Sit here awhile, as long as you need. Be washed. Breathe. Receive Jesus. Let Him capture your tears. Receive Peace.

28

LETTING GO OF CONTROL

*O*ne definition of *control* is "the power to influence or direct people's behaviour or the course of events."[1]

Holy Spirit began to speak to me further about my need for control, opening my eyes and my awareness to the many ways I have regularly attempted to exert it in my day-to-day life: with family, with others, and in any number of daily living situations.

One who has suffered trauma or abuse frequently has both conscious and subconscious need(s) to exert control (because they have been controlled) over every possible aspect of their life. Although originally for self-protection, this need spills over into every other area – how to do the smallest tasks, how to talk, how to live.... The need for safety and self-protection becomes a wounded, poisoned and ugly root to live life from.[2]

Holy Spirit OFTEN whispered, "Peace, be still; know I AM God. You can trust Me, you can let go now, I've got you. Underneath you are My everlasting arms, I will always catch you."

"I leave the gift of peace with you—my peace. Not the kind of fragile peace given by the world, but my perfect peace. Don't yield to fear or be troubled in your hearts—instead, be courageous!"

— JOHN 14:27, TPT

"Be still, and know that I am God..."

— PSALM 46:10A, ESV

"The eternal God is your refuge and dwelling place, and underneath are the everlasting arms; He drove the enemy before you and thrust them out, saying, Destroy!"

— DEUTERONOMY 33:27, AMPC

Activations For Learning to Be Loved

LETTING GO OF CONTROL

Selah ~

What more can you release control of?

———————

Pray the Word ~

"Thank You for Your constant assurances of Your love and Presence. Help me to let go, to quit trying to make my own way, control all situations, protect myself. Your Peace is always for me, not needing to be understood, only received. Thank You that You will ALWAYS catch me when I let go!"

———————

29

FORGIVENESS

I've left forgiveness until almost last but in reality, it is first –there can be no true healing begun or completed without forgiveness, no inner eyes to see until the biggest logjam is cleared away....

Psychologists generally define *forgiveness* as a conscious, deliberate decision to release feelings of resentment or vengeance toward a person or group who has harmed you, regardless of whether they actually deserve your forgiveness. Forgiveness does not mean forgetting, nor does it mean condoning or excusing offenses.[1]

Forgive[2] (verb)

- To grant pardon for or remission of (an offense, debt, etc.);
- To give up all claim on account of; remit (a debt, obligation, etc.);
- To grant pardon to (a person).

- Synonyms: pardon, absolution, exoneration, remission, dispensation, indulgence, clemency, mercy.

We humans wrestle with the whole topic. If someone is offended with us, we often don't see the big deal; if our conscience is pricked, we make excuses. Alternatively, we want forgiveness and understanding for ourselves but have a more difficult time passing it on to others. Self-pity may be our biggest deceiver. And self-righteousness. And pride.

A definition for forgiveness could be—giving up my right to hurt you for hurting me. It is impossible to live on this fallen planet without getting hurt, offended, misunderstood, lied to, and rejected. The word "forgive" means to wipe the slate clean, to pardon, to cancel a debt.[3]

In Matthew 18, Jesus tells a revealing story of a servant whose large debt to his merciful master King was cancelled – forgiven. But then this servant turned around and had a fellow servant with a small debt owed to him thrown in jail until all the second servant's debt was paid! Upon finding out what his forgiven servant had done, the master called the first servant back to his presence, calling his actions contemptible and wicked because he withheld mercy when he himself had been given it completely. And the master had his wicked servant "turned over to the torturers" until he paid all that he owed.[4] Jesus ended with these words:

> *"So also My heavenly Father will deal with every one of you if you do not freely forgive your brother from your heart his offenses."*
>
> — MATTHEW 18:35, AMPC

It is not that God is cranky, unkind, mean, or petty. He is just letting us see how great our debt is, and that He paid it Himself.

So great is God's love that Jesus, His Son—pure and holy and through Whom all creation was made—chose mockery, spitting, rejection, and derision. Despite our thumbed noses, He took the nails in His hands and feet and suffered a thorn crown to be jammed on his head from the very hands of those He had created – He, the spoken Creative Word of the Father, Who was One with Him in Spirit and His reflection! Jesus, Who said, "I only do what I see my Father doing! He who has seen me has seen the Father!"[5] chose to shed His pure blood as our sacrifice, paying the full debt to reconcile the whole creation to our Life-in-the-Garden-in-the-cool-of-the-day Father, in Whose presence it is impossible for darkness, for ANYthing unholy, to be present.

He really wants us with Him.

It is only by the gift of God that we come to recognise our own need of true and complete pardon, that our eyes are opened outward, that Light can begin to shine inward. Intended to live in relationship, to live loved by the Creator of all, we have instead lived separately, some to greater, others to lesser degrees; although truly, no evil is greater or lesser than another. All are evil; all deny Love.

I've seen inside my own soul and know I am capable of great offense. How can I judge another's depravity when I've seen my own and how far it could go if left unchecked? And I've prayed the holiest, most difficult prayer Jesus taught: Forgive me as I forgive others.

> *"Pray like this.... Forgive us the wrongs we have done as we ourselves release forgiveness to those who have wronged us."*
>
> — MATTHEW 6:9, 12, TPT

To Forgive and be Forgiven

It's so easy to see when we are wronged
not always so when we're the wrong-er

Especially the big stuff – boy can we see that:
Assault, abuse, adultery, lies,
Mockery – destroying being;
Taking advantage in any number of ways:
Theft of things, theft of soul, theft of life.

But what of hatred, resentment, disgust, dishonour?
What of roaring anger?
or filling emptiness with fill-in-the-blank stuff –
instead of turning to love?
What of hanging on to grievance –
righteously so! Look what they did! Despicable!

What of God-anger
when He didn't come through
when He "allowed" years and years and YEARS
of torment
WHY?
and His Words of love and 'trust Me' seem not only
     unbelievable,
but cruel?

What of unbelief – calling God a liar,
what of despair – ignoring His hand,
what of sarcasm, denigration,
using gift of words meant for creating
to destroy?

What of self-hatred, self-abuse, name-calling:

Sneering Stupid
Idiot!
Moron,
disrespecting
dishonouring
demoralising with almost every breath,
agreeing with darkness, believing the worst, every
    possible negative.

And believing there IS no darkness ...

What of soul-crushing starvation, denying life,
choosing blindly, only to meet immediate need, for
    escape
or indulgence;
or choosing self-protection instead of
in God we trust, like getting a complicated new – I
    CAN FIGURE IT OUT mySELF! instead of
making use of the "instructions for Life" clearly
    offered,
instead of hearing "Loved, cherished, a good plan, a
    way through, O honey
there are boundaries!"
not taking the Hand always reached out towards,
turning away from the One
Who has done everything
to make Himself known?

Yes, I do forgive the various ones who have brought
    me wounds but
most of all, I have needed to forgive me.
For believing lies.
And repeating them.

Freedom has been gained in
"Forgive
Release
and
Bless,"

in doing so, I am the most
forgiven
released
and
blessed
of all.

My Father, giving safety and honour to the wounded self, encouraged that extending forgiveness does not mean placing yourself back into unhealthy, unholy, dishonouring situations, with those who have not yet been heart-broken by their offenses ... yet, He does also whisper:

"The heartfelt compassion that hastens forgiveness matures when we see where our enemy cries."[6]

— BRENNAN MANNING

"Father forgive them; for they know not what they do..."

— LUKE 23:34, KJV

The reality is, it took time to learn new pathways of responding to life. The old familiar ones – fear, trying to control pretty much everything and everyone (ask my adult kids!), the feeling of being buried alive or chained to a huge cement block, false identity mantras, untrue beliefs about God – had no roots anymore, but they still had familiarity.

Learning to assimilate Truth and living from that place took time; almost two years of frequent trips to my Father's knee (sometimes moment-by-moment); often needing His encouragement; taking Jesus' still-warm, outstretched hand; His smile; His reminder of "in quietness and in trust..."[7]

Little by little, more and more, all that was left was stable ground. I now KNOW He is trustworthy, Good. He makes all things new.

All God's thoughts and plans for us – plans for good and not for evil, all His promised hope, good welfare, and peace – He did it all in Jesus. Free. Finished.

> "For I know the thoughts and plans that I have for you, says the Lord, thoughts and plans for welfare and peace and not for evil, to give you hope in your final outcome. Then you will call upon Me, and you will come and pray to Me, and I will hear and heed you. Then you will seek Me, inquire for, and require Me [as a vital necessity] and find Me when you search for Me with all your heart. I will be found by you, says the Lord, and I will release you from captivity ..."
>
> — JEREMIAH 29:11-14, AMPC

Activations For Learning to Be Loved

FORGIVENESS

Breath of Life ~

"Be still and KNOW Me!
It is finished.
It is accomplished.
It is all mine (and yours)
Now.
I've come to set all captives free."

"Receive My love today, deep within your being.
You never have to feel badly about needing to come to
Me often, frequently, ALWAYS for My help, for My
quiet, My love, My promises, needing to be reminded of
all these.

I MADE you for constant fellowship with Me, you were
designed for My Presence, My love, and it is never
wrong to be hungry and needful of Me – success is not
defined by needing to come to Me less!

Precious one, do not fear, and don't feel I AM angry

when I keep speaking "do not fear." Do not believe I AM
angry that I have to repeat Myself –I only remind you
that My love for you is complete, I AM with you and will
be with you every moment of your days – I will never
leave you uncovered, defenceless, helpless, for I AM
your Shield, your Refuge, your Help in time of need.

Coming to be encouraged in My love is simply as a child
knowing and going to her known and always needed
place of safety – into her Daddy's arms.
I AM building into you identity (that was lost), I AM
building into you Love, the Love that when fully
realised, unseats fear. Lay your head against My breast –
even as John the Beloved did – he knew My love was
complete, never-changing, something/Someone he
could always count on. In Me he found his rest. Blessed
are you as you follow his example, and his delight!

O My dear one, do not fear. I hold you! Do not fear the
world – I have overcome it and will keep you; I will
shelter you; I will give you songs of deliverance!

Stay hidden in Me. I do not call you out to slay dragons
in the public square – I call you to be a sanctuary – your
home, your very self. Can you do that?"

Selah ~

Has someone you love – perhaps yourself – been offended
against and it continues to eat at you, keeping you entrenched
in a particular period of time, believing there is little or no
recovery? Is fear (or any variety of debilitating responses, such

as rage, deep grief, or hopelessness) a frequent first reaction to any number of life's situations? Is there someone who needs to be forgiven? Maybe you?

Pray the Word ~

"Father, I need Your help to walk this out, to extend the forgiveness You have so graciously given me to another who has caused wounds and pain. Truly Your ways are not our ways. You know my freedom is chained up with unforgiveness, and that these chains bind me to the wounding and the wound-er forever, unless I can give forgiveness as You have given me. I have no defence before You. And I feel the huge links of the chain fall away.

Truly You are good, Father – Your plans are always for my good! Thank You for Jesus taking upon Himself, every curse, every weakness, every bit of sin and filth, every poverty that I have held in my heart. Thank You for taking all that has held me captive within from the acts of others, that has kept me from seeing Your face, from believing Your love. You counsel me strongly to be still, and to know You. I want to know You much more than I do now. I begin to see in that stillness that I will know You much more as I begin to express the grace You give to forgive all large and small offences against myself, and receive the greater grace of Your forgiveness for me."

30

SANCTUARY

*C*ontemplating **sanctuary**, I realise the fact of it is determined not by the location, or the structure of place, or props prepared, nor even by the longing of the one hoping, inviting, but by Who is present.

Sanctuary (noun)

- A consecrated place;
- A place of refuge and protection.[1]
- A sacred or holy place.[2]

WHO IS PRESENT

I just make space,
let You BE...

And ALL
is Consecrated.
Holy
Sacred

Sanctuary[3]

in me.

"*Have you forgotten that your body is now the sacred temple of the Spirit of Holiness, who lives in you? You don't belong to yourself any longer, for the gift of God, the Holy Spirit, lives inside your sanctuary.*"

— 1 CORINTHIANS 6:19, TPT

Activations For Learning to Be Loved

SANCTUARY

Selah ~

Did you know you were created to be a sanctuary for the sacred Presence of the Living God? For His Holiness to fill your being? Are you not all the way clear of the rubble that still seems to take up so much space within? still not quite able to breathe deep?

Can you receive the gift that there is no condemnation, only invitation - to Be Loved? His love will do the needed cleansing of His sanctuary (see John 17:17).

On That Note ~

Open Up Let the Light In by Steffany Gretzinger/Bethel Music

Pray the Word ~

"May Psalm 51:7 (TPT) be the prayer of your heart: 'Purify my conscience! Make this leper clean again! Wash me in your love until I

am pure in heart,' that I may be a living sanctuary for Your Presence."

— PART VI —

WORDS of WAITING

"Wait and hope for and expect the Lord; be brave and of good courage and let your heart be stout and enduring. Yes, wait for and hope for and expect the Lord!"

Psalm 27:14 (AMPC)

31

LIMINAL MOMENTS

*H*aving received so much in revelation and understanding of the bent and broken place I'd lived from for so long, and having begun to receive healing, promise, and calling on the other side of it, I was puzzled and frustrated that there still seemed much in the way of actually living free of it; still much that was weighty in spirit and unclear.

Nestled in the forest northwest of Cochrane, Alberta, Kings Fold Retreat Centre provides quiet space for listening, for contemplation, for hearing the voice of God. In September 2016, Grant and I took part in a one-day retreat that was offered, led in part by a young man who lived in community there. He shared a poem which was written by Warren Lynn:

> *This is a liminal moment;*
> *a threshold between what was, and is yet to be.*
> *Melancholy emerges in these days of human living,*
> *just as naturally as morning fog*
> *upon a lake too warm for the surrounding air.*

It is time to settle in to our unsettled lives.
Accept change like tamaracks consent to the seasonal
  loss of their needles.
Let our own turning move us to
Truth more lasting than fair weather.
Let Autumn be our guide.
Let Autumn prepare us for any darkness ahead.
Let Autumn teach us it is ok to let go. [1]

Liminal[2] (adjective)

- Relating to a transitional or initial stage of a process;

- Occupying a position at, or on both sides of, a boundary or threshold.

In anthropology, *liminality* (from the Latin word līmen, meaning "a threshold") is the quality of ambiguity or disorientation that occurs in the middle stage of rites, when participants no longer hold their pre-ritual status but have not yet begun the transition to the status they will hold when the rite is complete. During a rite's liminal stage, participants "stand at the threshold" between their previous way of structuring their identity, time, or community, and a new way, which the rite establishes.[3]

Threshold (noun)

- The entrance or start of something.[4]

- A boundary beyond which a radically different state of affairs exists.[5]

- A threshold is what you step across when you enter a room. A threshold takes you from one place into another, and when you're about to start something new, you're also on a threshold;

- The starting point for a new state or experience.[6]

Holy Spirit quickened the words *liminal* and *threshold* deeply into my heart, leading me to contemplate them deeply. First, I had to look up their meanings. I had a good idea of what *threshold* meant, but little understanding of *liminal*. The "ambiguity and disorientation" of the liminal stage noted in the definition above witnessed well. It really did feel like a time of transition, a place on "both sides of a boundary, a threshold." And a threshold is an exciting place to be, a ready-to-step-off-of-point into new and exciting opportunities! I actually heard great promise in *liminal* and *threshold* – there is definitely a something coming, the fruit of hope, the good plans of God. I'm just about there, almost ready to step into it...but it's unclear, and it's not quite here now... Oh, and before Life, comes Death.

Living on the Threshold

Wouldn't you think that living on the threshold of something you've been longing for over the course of many years, something that you have begun to have a sense of and even to see – wouldn't you expect that to be exciting? Exhilarating even? With its fresh crisp air, vibrant colours, scent of falling leaves, and apples and crabapples ready to be harvested, autumn had long been my favourite season. It was always invigorating. But that year I experienced autumn as a time of dryness: leaves falling, death, decay, barren dehydrated emptiness, no colour at all, devoid of life.

Yes, there was a liminal sense of something good pending far ahead, but not anywhere in sight. I was stopped between what was past and what was still ahead, not yet feeling like a threshold was opening up to somewhere. Continuing to contemplate and learn from Holy Spirit's lessons stirred by the poem at the Cochrane retreat, I asked God what I, like the leaves of autumn, needed to let go of, to release.

"What dead things am I hanging on to?"

I heard *once again*, "Control, planning, having to know, making contingencies for what is (or may be) coming."

"What am I to receive?" I wanted to know. "What is being given?"

"Now.
You are called to the NOW.
to the Rest of Now – this particular exact moment, right Now.
to the Trust of Now Only
to the Freedom of Now Only – no need to plan, to prepare, to do, make everything work out, or do the right thing. Just live NOW. Today.
Accept what is without judging it. Receive, recognise, and allow 'melancholy.' Do not be afraid of it; taste it, feel it, recognise it for what it is: a response emotion. Allow yourself to feel,
and not be afraid."

Activations For Learning to Be Loved

LIMINAL MOMENTS

Breath of Life ~

"Accept yourself where you are.

Accept where you are on your Emmaus Road – it is not failure. This is simply where you are, and I walk with you.

Accept that your body is fatigued – overstretched, and has been for quite some time. And it will take some time (quite!) for recovery. Don't force it into quick come-back. Receive the rest your BODY needs.

I'll meet you there.

Accept where your SOUL is – only just learning of possibility, only just beginning to receive affirmation, only just beginning to know love, just beginning to open up, unfold, to allow being held, given freedom.

Accept where you are in SPIRIT, in 'ministry,' in wisdom or lack of it,

in gifts or lack of,
less far along than you would like.

Accept where you ARE.
Let go of the rest."

Selah ~

Are you caught in a season of liminal, of in between one season and the next? Are you sensing there is a threshold to an exciting new chapter in your life ahead, but it's not quite in sight, and it's been feeling too long in coming? Can you take advantage of this liminal, threshold, waiting season to continue to press in to be still and quiet and to let go of needing to know? Can you choose to trust, to allow your own soul to be nurtured, fed, restored? Is there something you need to let go of? Could it be the need to see? Can you shed being consumed with living in the past or needing to experience the hoped for future and just live Today, right Now?

Pray the Word ~

"Father, You amaze me with Your continuing Grace for me – always speaking Rest, reminding that Your way is easy, light. Help me in these days that feel like You have walled me in, to see that these days are gifts too, with no pressure. I am learning to sit quiet, learning Trust yes, but also learning the pace of Your footsteps – never rushed, never late. Help me to receive all You want to give in this seemingly in between but very valuable time."

32

MELANCHOLY MOMENTS

*E*xperiencing melancholic moments is simply part of our journey at times, especially in seasons of letting go.

Melancholy[1] (adjective)

- Sad, sorrowful, desolate, melancholic, mournful, lugubrious, gloomy, pensive, despondent, dejected, depressed, depressing, down, downhearted, downcast, disconsolate, glum, sunk in gloom, miserable, wretched, dismal, dispirited, discouraged, low, in low spirits, in the doldrums, blue, morose, funereal, woeful, woebegone, doleful, wistful, unhappy, joyless, heavy-hearted, low-spirited, sombre, defeatist, pessimistic.

It may be helpful to be aware of the context of these words of liminal moment, threshold, melancholic, letting-go time. I had been experiencing challenges in my physical health and strength for some time. Additionally, we have four adult chil-

212 | LEARNING TO BE LOVED

dren, several of whom were experiencing crises in their lives, and we had our first new infant grandchild with all the joys and changes that grand life event brings! Plus, Grant and I were part of a community of people who were in the midst of GREAT upheavals/challenges that were often difficult to navigate.

The thing that Holy Spirit encouraged me with in this time is that feeling melancholy or sad is not faithless. Rather, it is an emotional response to long, drawn-out, difficult events while you are still going through them, when you cannot yet see what is on the other side. It is a weary body and mind and spirit - with valid reasons for being so...

While at Kings Fold that day of the retreat, I had entered a small chapel which was set alone among the trees at the top of a high cliff overlooking the Ghost River. There was only a large Bible on a stand across from the door and a couple of functional chairs.

I pondered what to read and heard, "Psalm 139." As I read once again through this Psalm that had already given much encouragement, affirming my own marvellously made-ness and the lover of my soul's ALWAYS Presence—OH! My breath got shocked away, my lungs flattened! OH! You were there all along! It was YOU I was fighting all along! All my life, it was YOU calling, arms outstretched to welcome me in, to give relief, to saturate in rest! But I would NOT! COULD not...and instead I wept, strove, pushed away Your every gentle attempt, and felt constantly all alone. I didn't KNOW! It was YOU!

FINALLY AT HOME

"You knew me then. You know me now.
Your love wraps me round

soft
thick
warm,

nowhere an opening for a sharp object to poke in, ...
  unless I walk away, forgetting ...

Keep me here. I am so, so finally at home.
Now here."

———

"Is there any place I can go to avoid your Spirit? to be out of your sight? If I climb to the sky, you're there! If I go underground, you're there! If I flew on morning's wings to the far western horizon, You'd find me in a minute—you're already there waiting!

Then I said to myself, "Oh, he even sees me in the dark! At night I'm immersed in the light!" It's a fact: darkness isn't dark to you; night and day, darkness and light, they're all the same to you.

You shaped me first inside, then out; you formed me in my mother's womb. I thank you, High God—you're breathtaking! Body and soul, I am marvelously made! I worship in adoration—what a creation! You know me inside and out, you know every bone in my body..."

— PSALM 139:7-15A, MSG

———

Through these liminal/threshold days, many times over, Abba Father (being present to me as comforting Daddy God) continued to whisper to me of His constant presence, His love, and His encouragement to trust Him. He wanted me to not respond to the needs of others—HE would see to their needs. He continually reminded me to allow Him to carry me, to let go of ALL dead things and simply lay back into Him.

It was during one of these many times of His loving "heldness" that I actually saw myself being absorbed into His chest cavity, into His heart, and there was no shame, no comparison, no fear, no doubt, no loneliness there. And from then on, that is where I lived, hidden, safe, held, strengthened, known.

I see this picture frequently: my "little me," the not-quite-fully-healed little girl's heart that He was loving especially, holding, hiding, healing. You can see from Holy Spirit's continuous repeating the same whispers over and over, over the space of years dear reader, that I am obviously a VERY SLOW LEARNER! Be encouraged! Clearly, He never gives up on us. And He is thorough.

Let Go of Dead Things

Autumn (the season of change) this particular year seen as the season of death.

"But," Jesus whispered, "How about it is the season of letting go of dead things? How about the seed that falls into the ground and dies, getting an opportunity to SPROUT and reproduce many times over, in time bringing fruitful abundance??!!"

> *"Listen carefully: Unless a grain of wheat is buried in the ground, dead to the world, it is never any more than a grain of wheat. But if it is buried, it sprouts and reproduces itself many times over. In the same way, anyone who holds on to life just as it is destroys that life. But if you let it go, reckless in your love, you'll have it forever, real and eternal."*

> — JOHN 12:24-25, MSG

Letting Go

In this

time of falling,

like   dead   leaves from   the sky,

old   deaths

        surprisingly   full   of   life,   seeking   to
spread

  the   grave   further
now .... yet

somehow   there   is ? ...

Trust ?   I   feel

     like   I

am

   dying,

  that   much   is   dead

already,

has   been   for

60   years -   Are   You   bringing

these things   to   life   so   they

can   have   a   proper

             b u r I a l?

"Why would you ever complain, O Jacob, or, whine, Israel (Janis, ANYONE), *saying, "God has lost track of me. He doesn't care what happens to me?"*

Don't you know anything? Haven't you been listening? God doesn't come and go. God lasts. He's Creator of all you can see or imagine. He doesn't get tired out, doesn't pause to catch his breath. And he knows everything, inside and out.

He energizes those who get tired, gives fresh strength to dropouts. For even young people tire and drop out, young folk in their prime stumble and fall. But those who wait upon God get fresh strength.

They spread their wings and soar like eagles, They run and don't get tired, they walk and don't lag behind."

— ISAIAH 40:27-31, MSG, EMPHASIS ADDED

"Those who sow with tears will reap with songs of joy. Those who go out weeping, carrying seed to sow, will return with songs of joy, carrying sheaves with them."

— PSALM 126:5-6, NIV

Activations For Learning to Be Loved

MELANCHOLY MOMENTS

Breath of Life ~

"Rest in Me, My beloved, My delight is in you. Simply let Me hold you, My Pea, My dear one. Be held.

Your spirit has been as a bruised reed, a dimly burning wick, and I will not break or quench you, I will restore you. I will refresh you, only keep true to Me, look at Me, your hand in Mine – I will bring you through – through the storm, the wind, the waves, and the fire.[2]

I want to bring you alive – fully alive. And that will happen as you lay back into My Son, be absorbed into Him completely, allow yourself to be loved, cherished, with no requirement but to BE.

There is no time limit.

My yoke for you, for all, is so easy, so light, you would have no sense or awareness that there IS a yoke, for in it you are released to rest, to fly, to listen to be: no encumbrances, no condemnations, no ignoring, no failure –

only rest
only joy
only Grace.

No more working for what is free!"

Selah ~

Are your hands and heart too full of dead things to be able to receive anything else? Are you willing to let go of what is so familiar, that even though it's dead, has been at least something known and therefore comfortable, like a ragged old shoe? What might some of those dead things be? Does terror rise up at thoughts there may be nothing ahead to fill the place that will be emptied?

On That Note ~

Undone by Kim Walker-Smith/Jesus Culture

Pray the Word ~

"O my Father! You are opening my eyes to see that I have had Your provision and love always, I just didn't see it. I didn't recognise You! I didn't open my hands and heart to receive what was right in front of me, what I've longed for all my life, that was offered in Your tenderness and power from the very beginning.

Forgive me for thinking that You did not care about me. Thank You for persisting in drawing me into wholeness, that I may see You, know You. Thank You that You draw me to a wide, solid, sound foundation to live my life from, that You call me to live in each moment, Your NOW. Help me to know what things I am hanging onto that are actually dried up and dead, keeping me from moving toward Life.

Thank You that as I let go, even letting those dried up kernels be buried in the ground, that You will raise up a harvest of righteousness, of abundant fruit, and You will put new songs in my heart, songs of praise, and laughter!"

— PART VII —

WORDS of PROMISE

Not one promise from God is empty of power, for nothing is impossible with God!

Luke 1:37, TPT

For all of God's promises have been fulfilled in Christ with a resounding "Yes!" And through Christ, our "Amen" (which means "Yes") ascends to God for his glory.

2 Corinthians 1:20, NIV

33

A DOVE

*D*uring a lovely time of soaking in His Presence in October 2016, I saw a dove released. Rising up, it flew around lightly and softly. I asked my Father what He wanted me to know about the dove.

He spoke to me:

- The dove is a symbol of purity, of quiet, of gentleness, of anointing.
- The dove is a symbol of My Presence and My peace.
- The dove is otherworldly: not disturbed by storms or strong wind currents, it remains quiet in itself.
- The dove has deep knowing within it, and though quiet, sees clearly and knows instinctively where to go, where to alight.
- The presence of a dove changes the atmosphere – it is as if all motion stops, breath is held. There is recognition of Presence.

I was reminded of instances of a dove in Scripture. Noah released a dove several times to find land after the flood in Genesis 8:8-12. When Jesus was baptised by John, a dove – symbol of the Holy Spirit – alighted upon Him.[1]

"O, that I had wings like a dove ..."

— PSALM 55:6, NRSV

"... the wings of a dove covered with silver, its pinions with shimmering gold ..."

— PSALM 68:13, ESV

"O my dove, in the clefts of the rock, ... let me see your face ... hear your voice ..."

— SONG OF SONGS 2:14, ESV

A dove is used as a term of endearment...and I heard:

"My anointing on and within you, My daughter, is the dove of peace – carrier, expression, of My presence. Where you go, My quiet within you shall change the atmosphere. You are being made whole. You are receiving grace to listen and recognise boundaries of love and care, wisdom, of not being distracted and over-taken by what you are not meant to be involved with. When Jesus walked this earth there were many He did NOT see and heal. His task and call were specific, limited to His human form.

I grace you My daughter with My Spirit as a dove. You shall have wings, light, transcendent, often specific direction, but sometimes general too. Keep separated to Me and I will guide you. I always have enough for everyone, and those you are not called to care for will be met in other ways.

I love you My little dove, and I am so well pleased when you capture My freedom and live in it. I release to you My Breath, My very Life Presence, the grace to float on quiet currents of Breeze – sensitive, soft to My inclination and direction, never moving too fast or erratically, but purposefully, quietly, unobtrusively."

Over and over, days and months into the following year, my Father continued to speak. He called to me, reminding me of His Peace, His easy yoke, His light burden, and His promises. He softly reminded me to continue letting go of dead things, not laying down with them.

I frequently heard His encouragement that the vision, the promise of "past the threshold into the new land, the Promised Land to be occupied," awaited an appointed time and though it tarried, though it seemed way overlong in coming, to wait for it, wait for it – it would surely come.[2] He was bringing me to the very end of pushing and striving; teaching me to simply be, to simply stand, hands empty and open, releasing everything in trust.

Promise[3] (noun)

- A declaration or assurance that one will do something or that a particular thing will happen.

"So now we must cling tightly to the hope that lives within us, knowing that God always keeps his promises....You need the strength of endurance to reveal the poetry of God's will and then you receive the promise in full."

— HEBREWS 10:23,36, TPT

Activations For Learning to Be Loved

PROMISE

Selah ~

Where are you in the waiting, in having a growing sense of who you are (and will be) in God's eyes, and what He is bringing you to? What words of promise have you heard? Did you know that a longing heart has a promise attached to it?

Pray the Word ~

"My Jesus, thank You that Your Kingdom is not of this world, that You speak to the deep places of my being. Thank You for grace to see further how You see me, what Your dreams and possibilities are for me. Thank You for the deep grounding peace of Your promises and that, if I have not yet seen my longings and hopes fulfilled, it is because the appointed time has not arrived yet. All my times are in Your hands, and You are Good! I say 'Yes' to all You see and say for me. I trust You for Your appointed time for everything concerning me."

34

IT'S TIME

*O*ne day, after a year (seemingly a lifetime) of waiting, I read from *I Hear His Whisper* by Brian Simmons:

"I run with passion into his abundance so that I may reach the purpose that Jesus Christ has called me to fulfill and wants me to discover. I don't depend on my own strength to accomplish this; however I do have one compelling focus: I forget all of the past as I fasten my heart to the future instead. I run straight for the divine invitation of reaching the heavenly goal and gaining the victory-prize through the anointing of Jesus."

— PHILIPPIANS 3:12-14, TPT

Brian's Holy Spirit-led challenge encouraged me to pray, "Where are You calling me to move forward today? I know You will meet me as I step out into new territory."[1]

I heard in my spirit: "It is time to face forward. Forget the past."

The healing season was over, finito! Face forward! It was time to step over the threshold, into His next. The foundation was firmly restored. Holy Spirit reminded me of the first prophetic word I was conscious of receiving, given by a friend back in April of 2011. It was the word that truly began my healing, bringing a solid anchor of HOPE:

> "God sees far deeper than we do and is now in process of drawing you with His grace to not let the past define you. And with that comes permission to "let go" and "become" because He was, is and will ever be. He is going to give you eyes to see who you are becoming (as you see Him), a woman of surrender, of blessing others, of carrying the heartbeat of God."[2]

"Let go" was there all along! And "become!" And "carry His heart!" I melted in worship. I'd turned the corner, crossed the threshold. He had said many times: "My Faithfulness surrounds you as a Shield. You have all you need. Always."

And I knew it was so.

Jesus and I walked and chatted, delighted in each other; we sang and danced together as in flowered fields, lay still in lush pastures watching cloud shapes in the sky. And He led me through what were still very deep waters in life circumstance, but His Peace began being more and more naturally mine. He called me to lay on my Father's altar the sacrifice of every heart concern I had, to release every one of those "challenging life situations," to lay them down completely, to TRUST HIM. And He whispered: "What has seemed a wall will become a way. And the way is JOY."

> *"Do not [earnestly] remember the former things; neither consider the things of old. Behold, I am doing a new thing! Now it springs forth; do you not perceive and know it and will you not give heed to*

it? I will even make a way in the wilderness and rivers in the desert."

— ISAIAH 43:18-19, AMPC

Activations For Learning to Be Loved

IT'S TIME

Selah ~

Are you running with passion towards the abundance God has for you? Have you heard the word to "forget the former things?" Are you willing? Is it time?

Pray the Word ~

"My Jesus, how I love You. You fill me up with Your presence, Your joy, Your promises, the absolute knowing that You are able to make ways in 'the wilderness' – the places where I have gotten lost and wandered and not been able to see. You make rivers of refreshing Life in the desert times, transforming them. You are always moving forward, bringing to new things! Grant me grace to let go of ALL the former things, everything that clings that has had me looking back-wards, that keeps me from moving forward. I put my hand in Yours. Let's go!"

35

JOY

*H*is surprise gift is joy: over and over repeated joy! In everything, everywhere, every trial, every puzzling circumstance, every difficulty we live with, whether illness, rejection, lack, and more. "For the joy set before Him, Jesus endured the cross" (Hebrews 12:2), and because He did, we are left with the fruit of His offering – we are LOVED! There is always "joy set before" us! ALWAYS! The healthiest, truest, most life-giving and life-restoring response we can give Him is joy expressed in thanksgiving, releasing trust, a quiet heart at rest in His.

Joy[1] (noun)

- The emotion of great delight or happiness caused by something exceptionally good or satisfying; keen pleasure; elation.

New eyes to see.

"We look away from the natural realm and we fasten our gaze onto Jesus who birthed faith within us and who leads us forward into faith's perfection. His example is this: Because <u>his heart was focused on the joy</u> of knowing that you would be his, he endured the agony of the cross and conquered its humiliation, and now sits exalted at the right hand of the throne of God!"

— HEBREWS 12:2, TPT, EMPHASIS ADDED

"Consider it a sheer gift (JOY^2), friends, when tests and challenges come at you from all sides. You know that under pressure, your faith-life is forced into the open and shows its true colors. So don't try to get out of anything prematurely. Let it do its work so you become mature and well-developed, not deficient in any way."

— JAMES 1:2-3, MSG

"I've told you these things for a purpose THAT MY JOY MIGHT BE YOUR JOY, and YOUR JOY WHOLLY MATURE!"

— JOHN 15:11, MSG, EMPHASIS ADDED

"Count it ALL JOY ...!"

— JAMES 1:2, RSV, EMPHASIS ADDED

Activations For Learning to Be Loved

JOY

Selah ~

Have you recognised the invitation to mature faith? To joy? To consider every challenge and difficulty an opportunity for growth into maturity?

Pray the Word ~

"Thank You Father for Your pure, joyful heart, and that You so patiently lead me out of death into life, out of sorrow into joy. Thank You that You do not want me to remain an infant in Your Kingdom, that You want to grow and mature me in You, in trust, in knowing the freedom and transforming power of Your Kingdom that uses absolutely everything in my life to reveal Who You are and who I am in You. When things are tough, help me – like Jesus – to focus on the coming joy and choose to begin to live in it now!"

36

GROWING IN THE GIFT

One sunny Sunday afternoon when I was about 5, while all the rest of my family were napping or elsewhere, I came across an absolutely beautiful soft bronzy-red leather coat laying in soft tissue in a newly opened box. I LOVED it! And I thought it was mine.

I put it on and went walking down our neighbourhood street in the sunshine. I still remember the glowing feeling of joy, the deep sense of having received a precious gift. My heart was FULL, THANKFUL!

Of course, when I returned home, I was told it was NOT my leather coat, it was my mom's new leather jacket. I remember the extreme sense of loss, going into my room, absolutely desolate within. I believe now this quite likely began the seed of a false belief, the negative expectation – that nothing good is or ever will be, for me. And throughout the years, there were many very special, lovely things that came but ended up being taken away, lost.

In 2016, Jesus was telling me that I'd "grown into my leather coat." It was for me after all – I'd just been too small at the time to wear it!

He has many more wonderful gifts to grow into ...

> "*I waited patiently* (well, truth be told, not always so!) *and expectantly for the Lord; and He inclined to me and heard my cry. He drew me up out of a horrible pit [a pit of tumult and of destruction], out of the miry clay (froth and slime), and set my feet upon a rock, steadying my steps and establishing my goings. And He has put a new song in my mouth, a song of praise to our God. Many shall see and fear (revere and worship) and put their trust and confident reliance in the Lord.*"
>
> — PSALM 40:1-3, AMPC, INSERT ADDED

Activations For Learning to Be Loved

GROWING INTO THE GIFT

Breath of Life ~

> "Precious Beloved, God's gifts of Word and words, of
> Breath and Life, Delight and Promise, are not just for
> me. In whatever state or situation you find yourself in,
> whatever life you have lived, whatever you have
> suffered, His gifts, healing and wholeness are yours, too.
>
> He longs to meet with you right in the centre of it all
> and bring you into all you were created to be."

Selah ~

Have you had glimpses or even senses of joy, only to have them
snatched away? Is it possible they were moments foreshad-
owing your coming inheritance, the beginning of your promise? God plans to breathe His Life into these things! Do you
remember Joseph and his dreams of his brothers bowing down
to him, only to be hated by them, sold into slavery in Egypt?
Can you trust that God WILL bring about what your heart has
heard? Have you been waiting patiently, and not so patiently?

(You can find the full story of Joseph in Genesis 37-47.)

On That Note ~

Walk in the Promise by Jeremy Riddle/Bethel Music

Pray the Word ~

"Once again, my Father, You remind me that You are good, and that You work ALL things together for good, not just my small part. You draw me out of the deep miry pit and plant my feet on the solid ground of You.

Thank You that every one of Your gifts of Promise, everything that my heart has found life in − even if only briefly − has had Your YES in it, and it shall be so, because Jesus is Your Yes and Amen!"[1]

— Part VIII —

WORDS of LIFE

*"Arise [from the depression and prostration in which
circumstances have kept you—rise to a new life]! Shine (be
radiant with the glory of the Lord), for your light has come,
and the glory of the Lord has risen upon you!"*

Isaiah 60:1, AMPC

"I AM LIFE!"

from John 14:6, AMPC

EXPECTATIONS

One day I was questioning my Father about the *why* of a number of events and situations in which things were basically falling apart, causing a lot of disturbance and sorrow – wrangling trauma even – for many (and sometimes just me). It seemed as if nothing was working out as anticipated, prayed, dreamed, or longed for in any sphere.

I heard:

> "My lovely one! My beloved ~ peace to your soul! It's about expectations.
>
> Don't have any.
>
> When you have expectations (for people or situations for out-workings), you limit Me and you limit yourself from receiving what IS and finding Me, and My Kingdom, in the midst of it.
>
> This is what happened: There were many varied expec-

tations and when they were not met there were all manner of reactions – irritation, disappointment, disturbed spirit, anger, loss of quiet and intimacy with Me, self-pity, self-righteousness, judgement and criticism – the opposite of love, peace and well-being.

I desire all My children to have only one expectation – that there I AM in the midst of them. Expect to hear Me, to meet with Me, whatever the outward situation is, no matter the disturbance or disappointment caused by the actions of others. Meet with ME. Hear ME.
I AM peace, I AM joy, I AM patience, kindness, LOVE.

People and situations, even those you love best and easiest, will sooner or later disappoint you, and you them. The question is, what do you want to grow into in response?

Choose Me.
Choose life.
Choose grace.
Choose Forgiveness.
Choose to Trust Me.
Choose Love.

Look for what I AM doing. And you shall be in freedom and Joy! ALWAYS. Let your only expectation be My Presence. THAT is always so!"

Expectation[1] (noun)

- A strong belief that something will happen or be the case in the future.

- A belief that someone will or should achieve something.

- Synonyms: supposition, assumption, presumption, conjecture, surmise, calculation, prediction.

What Holy Spirit was speaking here reminded me of something I had come across years before and had been challenged and exhilarated by: a quote written by Larry Hein, (once spiritual director to Brennan Manning):

> May all your expectations be frustrated, may all your plans be thwarted, may all your desires be withered into nothingness, that you may experience the powerlessness and poverty of a child and sing and dance in the love of God who is Father, Son, and Spirit.[2]

It's something to chew on, isn't it? It is something to listen in for – frustrated expectations? Thwarted plans? Withered-to-nothingness desires?

God may shine His light on some things that we've been hanging onto that have kept us bound and the question becomes, are we willing to let them go? Can I trust God for better than what I think is right? Can I trust Him to love me?

In this, I heard great freedom: to not have to figure anything out, to not have to figure out 'right' desires and prayers even, but rather to live in the freedom of being a truly loved and cherished child of God, Who has revealed Himself as Abba Father, Saviour-Redeemer-Friend, Helper, Teacher, Fruit- and Gift-Anointer.

When we have expectations, we limit God and people to the small box of what we can think is possible. We show a certain arrogance in assuming we know what is best for other people and situations. However, when we release those expectations we are free to sing and dance, to trust Him for what we cannot fully see, and God is free to bring His goodness (which is frequently far beyond our imagining).

"Jesus Christ is the same yesterday and today and forever."

— HEBREWS 13:8, NIV

"...lo, I am with you always, even to the end of the age."

— MATTHEW 28:20, NASB

Activations For Learning to Be Loved

EXPECTATIONS

Selah ~

Are there any unmet expectations which come to mind that are raising up a stink in your being and causing turmoil, maybe keeping you from seeing what IS being given in place of what you expected? Has anyone disappointed you with their choices? Failed to be who you hoped they would be or to do what you hoped they would do? Any situations not what you expected? Can you dance on them?

Pray the Word ~

"O God, deliver me from having expectations of others, of myself, or of situations and outcomes of hopes and prayers even. Thank You that You never change, I can count on You. You are always trustworthy, faithful, good. And You have promised You are always with me. I need to know nothing else."

38

REST (AGAIN)…AND SLAYING GIANTS

One day, having come to my prayer chair, heart ready to listen, I asked: "What do You want me to focus on today? What ground to gain?" This is what I heard:

"Rest: living in My rest. Nothing to disturb you because you are always in My rest, being yoked with Me.[1] Gaining the ground of REST will make you fearless, courageous, quiet to hear, quick to perceive, and full to release My Presence.

Gaining the ground of REST will give you a wide and strong foundation on which to live, not just to stand. Everything that comes after will be easy. So do not rush the learning: live it, enjoy it, experience it! REST is never to be lost once found. It is the cornerstone of peace, which is the bedrock of My Kingdom, for I am not disturbed and changeable, and My actions are not determined by emotion.

I live from the place of REST. I know Who I am. While

on earth in physical form, Jesus always lived from His REST in Me – He sought Me early in the day to be built up and nourished, replenishing His being in My Presence. It is in My REST that you experience My love. My love is unhurried and undisturbed. My love is freeing, releasing, uplifting, encouraging, warming, full of REST!

REST for the weary one.
REST and freedom for the captive in strife.
REST and hope for the hopeless.
REST and love for the rejected lonely one.
REST and peace for the fearful.
REST is foundational for Life.

Go back to Psalm 91 and receive more. You are recognising the different events and challenges in your life as presenting an opportunity to choose what I have been speaking into you. All are opportunities to Rest and in so doing, you will slay the giants of fear, disturbance, and doubt. Rise up fierce beloved, in My Rest! As you step into My Rest, you will become the giant, and what you thought was impossible to overcome, will be to you as small as a mouse. You take the steps and I will meet you easily in them. My yoke is easy, My burden light – REST for your soul. This is My Kingdom."

"The reverent, worshipful fear of the Lord leads to life, and he who has it RESTS satisfied; he cannot be visited with [actual] evil."

— PROVERBS 19:23, AMPC, EMPHASIS ADDED

Activations For Learning to Be Loved

REST... AND SLAY GIANTS

Selah ~

Is there a giant in your land that may be slain by choosing to Rest in the One Who loves you?

Pray the Word ~

"How I love You God, You Who are before all and in all things! You created the whole earth and everything in it! Thank You for loving me before I even knew You, before I loved You back. Thank You for inviting me into Your Presence, Your sanctuary of rest, Your heart. My holy Father, my dear Jesus, my Friend, thank You that living in Your rest, in the whole beauty and expanse of Who you are, makes me fierce against all giants that rise up against me, and they have no recourse but to fall, defeated."

39

SLOW DOWN—YOU MOVE TOO FAST

I love driving. I had a great teacher – my Dad! He loved driving and did a lot of it. He taught me all the skills, explained the whys behind the particular placement of traffic signs, how to drive on gravel and around graveled corners (although my first attempt landed us in the ditch). My Dad instilled in me a love for the dance of the drive!

He also exampled driving efficiently, such as avoiding heavy traffic (lots of side roads) and basically never EVER using your brakes unless absolutely necessary (it saves the brake pads). Part of it was a gift of awareness and paying attention, but part of it was, as any good card player knows (which he was), being two steps ahead of everyone around him.

He had that kind of keen mind. And part of it was a push to see how far he could go without stopping! I remember gazillions of times, Dad taking his foot off the gas pedal and coasting up to a red light, slower and slower, not wanting to put on the brakes and fully have to stop, slowly coasting further and further into the intersection – "Dad! Dad! DAD! STOP!!!" I remember the growing fear and tantalizing horror (mixed with excitement) to see how far he'd go and what would happen!

As a good student, I learned his techniques well and perhaps took them to the next level. I felt pretty assured of my skills. For years I liked to drive at the uppermost limit of the "10kph above maximum." At one point in my early years, one of my ambitions was to be a race car driver – my kids can attest to this! I was pretty impatient with other drivers who didn't drive correctly (according to the driver's manual, and me, of course), critiquing them constantly, out loud, always looking to get ahead or go around, frequently passing those who were impeding where I was going, breezily flying by, loving the dance and flow of the drive.

Now, Holy Spirit had spoken many times over the years regarding having His heart of charity, forgiveness, understanding, (etcetera, etcetera, etcetera!) for other drivers, and I really did move greatly in that direction. But, following the year of Liminal Moment—Threshold and preparing for stepping into New Territory, He began to actively deal with me in this area, with impact for every other aspect of my life.

He began to hem me in behind abnormally slow drivers for long periods of time with no way to get around them. "I'm going to be LATE," my brain would scream. "WHAT ARE YOU DOING DRIVING LIKE THAT?" I would mutter. "I'VE TIMED MY ARRIVAL TO THE VERY DOT OF TIME NECESSARY. WHAT'S THE MATTER WITH YOU?"

Hemmed in! And every single time I drove, hemmed in by VERY SLOW DRIVERS ON EVERY SIDE, I began to hear the words to a song. Holy Spirit brought Paul Simon's song, "Feelin' Groovy"[1] to my mind and spoke to me from the lyrics which talked about... You guessed it, *slowing down.*

For a YEAR.

It very quickly became a jolly happy recognition, and I'd laugh out loud at the impossible slooooooowness of the cars in front of and beside me, knowing my Abba Father was speaking directly to me. And I'd giggle and sing the song, over and over, "slow down," hearing it and knowing that it was about much more than my driving. It was about living – to stop pressing forward, always rushing to the next; it was about BE-ing in the moment – in rest and enjoyment, with a smile on my face and in my heart, living loved every second, paying attention, aware. It was about "cease striving," stillness, and knowing God.

He still sings it to me from time to time, and I relax and laugh and sing along with Him, "Feelin' groovy!"

During this same time, He also spoke to me about all my critiquing of other drivers, asking me to learn to let them be. It took a while. I'd start off my drive asking for His quiet heart, to not react against anyone else driving, to not make comments or criticise, and then within two minutes I would do just that. And I'd shake my head, disappointed in myself for failing that particular test. However, I started to enjoy this, knowing that good things were coming. I looked forward to beginning again the next day, challenging myself to see if I really could go without criticising, and it became another laughing fun thing!

There were quite a number of days that I got to the very last minute and let an exasperated critical word escape (e.g., "Really??? What on earth!!??), and I'd exclaim, "Dang it! Almost made it! Maybe tomorrow..." We still have opportunities to work on this together from time to time.

All this with my driving was not about driving, although that has improved immensely. It was highlighting the impatient, disrespectful, critical spirit that I carried, and making me aware of its reflection in how I responded to situations in other areas of life. With no condemnation I was invited into laughter, while at the same time being transformed in so much Love.

God never ever condemns. His Light brings revelation, and grace.

> *"The good person out of the good treasure of the heart produces good, and the evil person out of evil treasure produces evil; for it is out of the abundance of the heart that the mouth speaks."*
>
> — LUKE 6:45, NRSV

Activations For Learning to Be Loved

SLOW DOWN

Selah ~

Have you been feeling hemmed in by God? Frustrated? What might Holy Spirit be bringing that is not in your typical place of receiving? What may He be exposing, and wanting to lovingly hone into His beautiful likeness?

On That Note ~

The 59th Street Bridge Song (Feelin' Groovy) by Simon and Garfunkel

---

Pray the Word ~

"Jesus, thank You for always calling me to the "now" – to not be rushing on ahead, but to be present in each moment: no striving, being still, seeing with Your eyes, living in and releasing Your rest and Your enjoyment! Thank You for all the myriad ways that You speak and reveal Yourself and Your Kingdom. Thank You for revealing the issues of my heart in the Light of Your holiness. You are

always revealing Life if I will only pay attention, revealing where my heart has spoken out of death, what has not been from Your pure Living Water. Wash me clean, purify my heart. Please, give me ears that hear, eyes that see, so that I will not miss anything You want to bring to my understanding."

40

TIME

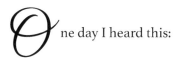ne day I heard this:

"Janis, I give you My strength, I give you My peace. It is a new season. You shall have strength for far more than ever before. Do not look ahead in the natural, on the basis of what has been in the past, for I tell you, I AM giving you new strength beyond what has been in the past. It shall be moment by moment, you shall not see ahead for it, cannot plan for it, simply trust I will give you all you need. It is a new day.

I shall give your body the rest you need to sustain you, yet it shall not be the rest of old – you shall simply depend on Me to give you all you need moment by moment. I AM your constant supply. When you look ahead in the natural you will say, "It is too much!" I say, do not look ahead – look at Me. BE, in Me. And I will take you ahead. I will meet you in each moment.

I AM bringing you into the place where you know that

all your times are in My hands. And you shall have no need to plan or weigh or balance, to look ahead and determine "if" – I shall be your provision all ways. That will be your dependency – ME – not your own strength or calculations!

You are being brought into the truth of the Word – "Do not say you will do such and such," but rather say "If the Lord wills, I shall ..."[1] because you shall know that your entire life shall be lived AS THE LORD WILLS – and I will take you places, and into situations and opportunities you have not dreamed of.

You shall live one moment at a time, and I will meet you in every moment. Every step shall be holy ground, for it shall all be in Me and where I AM is HOLY. Wherever you go, ground and lives, shall be consecrated to Me. And you shall know My rest and My JOY!"

TIME, aka Gift

Once a pressure: never enough, confining, defining
*   tyrant, needing to plan it, lists guiding, heart*
*   chiding, gotta use it use it WELL make the most*
*   of, don't waste*
TIME! ...
a bully not a playmate, not to enjoy but to dread
*   instead,*
*   deadlines, unseen but felt concrete BLOCK threat-*
*   ening to*
fall
snapping tense strung out thin nerves:
failed again, or
maybe not...

Now, ease! (when I remember) for You've sweetly
whispered: 'O My honey! All Your times are in
My hands! There's always enough! There's no
time limit, NO FAIL, only
 unforced rhythms of grace
aaaaahhhhh
I have more time now than ever before! more accom-
plished, more enjoyed, more
lived
each
moment
with a
smile
Time no longer tyrant but friend,
full of opportunity because
LOVE is trusted
to fill
all.
Now I go on exploits!
Every day.

Time (noun)

- The part of existence that is measured in minutes, days, years, etc.; or this process considered as a whole.[2]
- The indefinite continued progress of existence and events in the past, present, and future regarded as a whole.[3]

"My times are in your hands..."

— PSALM 31:15, NIV

Activations For Learning to Be Loved

TIME

Selah ~

How tightly are you bound to time? What rises up in you when you think of releasing time?

Pray the Word ~

"Dear God, I seem to frequently need this reminder – that all my times are in Your hands – You are Lord over all my moments, there is no need for flurry or distress. Thank You for taking me deeper and deeper into the Rest of knowing that ALL my times are in Your hands of Love. May I use the Time you give to me well, reflecting Your smile."

41

DANCING TRUST

*D*ance is "to move one's feet or body, or both, rhythmically in a pattern of steps, especially to the accompaniment of music."[1] In responding to the question, "What is full form dance?" Quora user, Ankita Vaibhav, said that "dance is an art which makes you happy and beautiful while dancing."[2]

Since 2014 or so the word *dance*, as well as the physical action of it, has particularly enthralled me. I only remember having a few tap dance lessons at our neighbourhood Community Hall when I was a child, and my failure to get past a dance audition when I was a teenager affirmed that I did not exhibit much natural skill. But my whole being has always responded to music – I cannot hear music without moving!

For years I'd grown up in one of the "frozen chosen" denominations as they were sometimes known, but when I came into a faith community that gave freedom for movement and dance, I came to life, responding to Spirit, feeling finally fully able to connect with and express my love for our incredible, holy, loving God.

In this new season of coming to Life, of seeming to receive lessons of spirit in practically everything, I was brought into a whole new recognition and experience of Dance, and I penned this:

When Is a Dance Not a Dance but Is Truly a Dance?!

When it's a call to a movement – not necessarily of
    feet or of limbs, (though that can be part),
but when it's an invitation to a movement of heart ~
to learn the steps to enter something wholly
    unknown, often jarring – like the samba after the
    waltz – not making any sense, awkward, irritat-
    ing, ears cannot even hear the beat of it or brain
    make sense of it, it's the exact opposite *of the*
    previous Dance ...
You thought you knew the language but even that's
    changed
and it takes a long while to recognise, recalibrate ...it's
    not about what you thought it was ...
Ahhhh....

Breath of Heaven

Interpreting Amy Grant's song, "Breath of Heaven," in dance movement for some ladies at a Christmas Tea, I came to recognise that the invitation was not about dancing. I know some were blessed, and in preparing I did recognise that we (His Lovers) are all Marys crying out for help to birth the Jesus we carry within through the outward expression of our lives. It became my prayer too.

But the invitation really was for me. "Come dance with **Me**," Jesus was saying. He didn't even mean *dance* the way I thought He meant, that I should get back into responding to Him and expressing my love and worship of Him to music through dancing, which at that time I had not done in a while. However, He meant for me to enter the movement of His breath in and through me, to learn better what that looks like...come in, come up. The "Dance of Life" as it is meant to be danced!

The month of preparing for dancing *Breath of Heaven* was the most profoundly significant revelation of His Presence, of His quiet, and of grace to trust that I'd ever experienced to date. Jesus kept telling me to trust Him as I awaited revelation of the movements to begin: Janis, who likes to plan early, well ahead of deadline need-to-be-ready-time, in order to enjoy the peace of the movements and grow in easy skill, naturally responding! But for over a month He gave nothing for movement, only quiet, only speaking "Trust Me," until I trusted that even if I heard or saw no direction at all except to stand still in His Presence as the music played, that would be enough.

He didn't begin to give the choreography until the very last night before and early morning of the day of presentation. The movements were simple and powerful, and moved me (and others) to tears.

Learning Trust

From this intensive, set apart time that was basically spent at the feet of Jesus, (Luke 10:38-42), I learned that I could trust God to the very last second of not seeing proof. It was the beginning of a whole new journey of dancing: living deeply trusting in a fully loved life.

Trust[3] (noun)

- Firm belief in the reliability, truth, or ability of someone or something.

Hannah Whitall Smith understood a deeply basic truth when she said, "It is a law of the spiritual life that every act of trust makes the next act less difficult. Trusting becomes like breathing, the natural unconsciousness of the redeemed soul."[4]

The invitation of God to enter the schoolroom of Trust, frequently sitting at the feet of Jesus to hear what He is saying [in the particular area] where trust is needed; fighting to choose trust though our whole being screams that only mayhem and disappointment, perhaps embarrassment and more will follow – this invitation is a holy one and if honored, will bear powerful fruit that never dies. And, if intentionally stepped into (because you REALLY want to hear and receive what Jesus has) the journey through this invitation most certainly makes it much easier to choose to trust God in any situation afterwards. You will have built a strong foundation of Trust, and every choice that follows continues to build on that foundation. Your life in Him will become a strong fortress, impregnable to assaults, fears, and unknowns. You will truly come to know, understand, and *experience* the Faithfulness of God!

In his book, *Ruthless Trust*, Brennan Manning wrote:

> Why does our trust offer such immense pleasure to God? Because trust is the preeminent expression of love. Thus it may mean more to Jesus when we say, "I trust You," than when we say, "I love You."[5]

I truly believe this. Love without trust says we don't really know the one we are professing to love, our love says that they may inspire hope, some experience of relationship, but we're not so sure they will be there for us in the tough times.

While every human being has the possibility of not being worthy of all our trust all the time, our holy living loving Creator, Redeemer, Sustainer most certainly is Worthy. Always! And it is in our own best interests to begin to mature, be built up and strengthened in the CORE of our being, that He is a good, faithful, loving God and Friend, that He uses Everything to our good, that He is creating a reflection of Himself in our lives so that others may see Him when they look at us.

Learning to Trust Him is learning a new needed language – one that will only make us stronger, take us higher and further, one that will give us wings far above any situation that attempts to threaten. Learning to say "I trust You, Jesus," is most definitely the truest expression of our love.

> *"Those who trust in, lean on, and confidently hope in the Lord are like Mount Zion, which cannot be moved but abides and stands fast forever."*
>
> — PSALM 125:1, AMPC

Activations For Learning to Be Loved

DANCING TRUST

Selah ~

Sit with it: being a Holy Mountain. Immovable, solid, stable, standing Strong, always: because you trust God!

Pray the Word ~

"LORD, You are my only Hope! I am learning to trust You and it is wonderfully strengthening! Grant me grace – Your powerful Presence — always to lean on You Who never changes, never moves, or shifts. Make me strong, steadfast, immovable, like You."

42

NEW CHOREOGRAPHY!

*L*iving knowing you are loved is a dance with new choreography.

Learning the steps of a new choreography, though sometimes challenging, can be fun! Of course, it was not really new, after all, since Jesus had been inviting me into it for years. I just had not been able to fully enter in due to being incredibly fearful, following old habits of orphaned response, or not under-standing or trusting His purity of heart and His determination for Life. However, He kept loving the "chunks" of ill-imposed life off of the (many) places where His intention for wholeness and beauty had been stolen.

It builds up – the filth and crud formed from my own fractured responses, from living life alongside broken people (each usually doing the best they can), and from listening to the liar who came to steal, kill, and destroy. Jesus keeps exposing and delivering, inviting us into grace-healing-freedom, and impossi-bilities became not only possible but reality. My whole being finally began hearing and receiving His love, beyond anything known, anticipated, or hoped for. It was pure and true.

Jesus knows who He made each of us to be and He is fierce for us to be free to live, knowing that when one of His beloveds lives truly, then all around us comes a circle of refreshing and further invitation into True for every other life coming in contact – it just happens! Kingdom comes.

Jesus is fierce for ALL!

Lungs fill deeply, release slowly. All of life, every situation, is invitation into His wholeness, His rest, His utter joy. We see through new eyes, and nothing looks like it once did! There are no walls, requirements, *musts* or *shoulds* when life is lived from within His heart.

Jesus keeps saying, "Follow your heart, for there I AM."

DANCING

The veil is torn
I see Your face
Your hand extended to embrace
my trembling self
Your eyes for me
are all I see
intent fierce tender strong
warm longing draws me safely in
harboured against within
Your arms Your breast
Home.
Home.
and in the stillness undisturbed yet comes a
whirling
twirling
swirling
laughter bubbling dancing over

meadows hills and
purple mountains
tumbling brooks shining stones beneath
water so brightly clear it hurts your eyes and cannot
    be stopped the Source will NOT
be held back!
the very flowers of the fields laughing alive
all mingling with Your own exuberant guffaws and
JOY!
Oh!
Oh the bliss!
who knew Adonai loved to DANCE
like this!!!!

"For in Him we live and move and have our being..."

— ACTS 17:28, NKJV

Activations For Learning to Be Loved

NEW CHOREOGRAPHY

Breath of Life ~

"Here we are beloved, learning what it is to take My hand, to forget about the steps of the old dance – the one you thought was Mine but was really rules and confined boxed requirements. But your heart has been for Me and you have continued seeking after Me, and your longing to know Me more deeply drew you in to discover that I am always for you, and dancing with you gives Me joy!

I love Dancing with you, for you are a willing and responsive partner, always desiring to learn and to follow in My steps, to be led, to receive whatever I want to give you, your ears always open to My whispers, your heart fierce for True. And I say to you – you who gives so much encouragement to others, to receive that same encouragement for yourself – go easy on yourself! My yoke, My invitation, is always easy, always light. The steps are really quite simple. You are learning what love is.

I dance with you in the place of unjust accusation. I

dance with you in the place of unmet expectations. I dance with you in the place of being unreceived. I dance with you in the place of unknowing. I dance with you in the place of not yet seeing the fulfillment of your heart's deep desires. I dance with you for joy!

I hold you in My Heart and together we dance in the Tabernacle opened to you by the sacrifice of My Son, in the flowered fields of refreshment, upon the mountains of resistance and upward to new heights, in the heavens and beyond the heavens!

You shall indeed see My Glory. You are learning to Fly!"

Selah ~

Would you like to dance with the Lord of Life? Are you ready to let Him lead?

On That Note ~

Come Away by Jesus Culture

Pray the Word ~

"O, yes – may all my movements be birthed in and led by You Jesus, King of Kings, Lord of Lords, Friend! May I always move to Your rhythm, the beat of your heart."

43

LIVE LOVED

"... in our faithful listening to God's Word, we often neglect his first word to us – the gift of ourselves to ourselves: our existence, our temperament, our personal history, our uniqueness, our flaws and foibles, our identity. Our very existence is one of the never-to-be-repeated ways God has chosen to express himself in space and time. Because we are made in God's image and likeness, you and I are yet another promise that he has made to the universe that he will continue to love it and care for it....

In patient endurance we wait for God to make clear what he wants to say through us. Such waiting demands not only alert attention but the courage to let ourselves be spoken. Such courage arises from unfailing trust in the wisdom of God, **who utters no false word.**

... How glorious the splendor of a human heart which trusts that it is loved..."[1] (emphasis mine)

I have come to truly trust that I am loved, and it is a whole new experience. (I actually thought I already did.) This realization dramatically altered the landscape of how I came to My Father's presence, that is, in desperate need – I realised that I don't ever need to be needy in that same way anymore! What does that look like?

O yes! Gratitude! Unforced rhythms of grace, easy, light,[2] whispers and leading each moment, rest, hidden, cared for, a Loved Daughter in freedom, soaring with no effort.[3]

Yes, there are times I need some reminding, but the pathway to the new place of trust and rest has become familiar, and I can enter in much quicker now. Over and over I hear His whisper, "Live loved today. Live loved [in this situation]. Live loved, My Pea! Live loved – I love you! Live loved!"

Truly living loved immediately removes tension from the body, mind, and spirit. It is impossible to be fearful, anxious, angry, or disturbed when we live in the knowledge and awareness of our beloved-ness. "Perfect love casts out fear" (1 John 4:17) really is true! Fear has nowhere to land when our hearts know we are perfectly never-to-be-left-alone loved!

From Orphans to Sons/Daughters

ORPHANS:

*don't even like themselves, comparing badly to most
    or conversely better than many,
can't, won't receive help, only see failure,
guard their hearts, hide them too, have long ago
    hidden them deep deep away,*

constricted by shame, inner accusation,
  condemnation;
live by rules, hate rules, require rules, it's the only
  way to know who loses, and it's always them;
strive for praise, long for praise, don't care if you don't
  praise, who cares what
you think?
crave peace, recognition, affirmation, freedom, love,
identity, approval, security, to be seen;
live constricted, resenting serving, everything is slav-
  ery, fighting always for scraps.
or not.
give up, only see lack, carry cart loads of self-pity;
need control for protection,
cannot trust, there's no one, nothing to trust;
live alone in the midst of many, eyes blinded, ears
  stopped up;
work for everything, nothing easy, all is a duty,
  required DOING;
are so tired, insist on loyalty, often give it but easily
  disappointed when not returned;
only see the worst, get comfort where they can,
live in poverty in the midst of abundance;
do not know they are loved.
I've been one.

Sons and Daughters:

live loved, giving no thought for their care: all is
*   provided,*
live free; eyes, thoughts, senses, fully responding to
*   whatever comes in the moment,*
hearts open to receive, live joyfully, filled with inter-
*   est, keenly learning,*
rest, fully trust, completely,
always;
no fear, only safety, there are no limits to love,
only warm guidance;
willingly serve without recognition,
always have a lap to sit on, a hand to hold, a safe
*   secret place to BE;*
forgive easily knowing they are forgiven, and
having been forgiven, they forgive -
no condemnation;
honour, knowing they are honoured,
can be hidden, knowing they are seen,
can be silent, knowing they are heard,
can love, knowing they are loved;
they find joy in the dancing, serving, waiting, even
*   mockery, curses, despisings;*
respond to all with joyful thankfulness in simplicity
*   or plenty;*
know Peace, ARE Peace;
have a massively enormous inheritance they receive
*   NOW because their testator has died (but lives!)*
I am one! I am becoming one! I am taking hold of
*   and learning how to BE one -*
Loved!

"Dwell in Me, and I will dwell in you. [Live in Me, and I will live in you.]"

— JOHN 15:4, AMPC

"I have told you these things, that My joy and delight may be in you, and that your joy and gladness may be of full measure and complete and overflowing!"

— JOHN 15:11, AMPC

"[Joyfully the radiant bride turned to him, the one altogether lovely, the chief among ten thousand to her soul, and with unconcealed eagerness to begin her life of sweet companionship with him, she answered] Make haste, my beloved, and come quickly, like a gazelle or a young hart [and take me to our waiting home] upon the mountains of spices!"

— SONG OF SONGS 8:14, AMPC

Activations For Learning to Be Loved

LIVE LOVED

Selah ~

What does it feel like to know you are loved? That you are God's one-of-a-kind-expression of His goodness, you are absolutely precious, and you are an integral, essential part of His gift to all His creation? How does that change how you can live today or tomorrow?

On That Note ~

The Bridegroom sings over His Bride (you! me!): *Isa's Song* by Laura Rhinehart

Pray the Word ~

"Jesus, Your goodness, Your hand reached out to me, Your invitation to live fully loved, in joy always, is so far beyond my comprehension! But, oh yes! I want to enter into Your dance, Your invitation to soar and to fly in Your freedom, living in Your beyond-understanding

delight. Thank You that You never stop inviting me to Your side, to Your care, to Your Love. You never condemn me, only encourage me, teaching me what it is to Be Loved...and how to live loved."

44

SOARING AND STILLNESS

$\mathcal{I}$saiah 40:31 promises soaring flight to those who learn to wait with and for God:

"But those who wait for Yahweh's grace will experience divine strength. They will rise up on soaring wings and fly like eagles, run their race without growing weary, and walk through life without giving up."

— ISAIAH 40:31, TPT

I know that it surely must be birthed in the foundational Word of the Good News, the finished work of Jesus the Christ. We cannot soar until we know what His death in our place on the Cross accomplished, what His resurrection from the grave released, what His Spirit poured out on the day of Pentecost for all to receive.

We cannot soar in our Father's freedom without being deeply grounded in Who He is, what His heart wants and what He has accomplished for His creation. When once we begin to truly know and receive THAT, our hearts and beings will just naturally begin to soar as we are overcome with wonder that a love and freedom and joy so great can be ours.

SOARING

I've found what is true, that
in order to soar,
fly high, leave the
shore,
to experience
MORE,
takes being more grounded
than
ever before.

Like the chicken and the egg, which comes first – soaring...or stillness? Throughout this season of learning more completely to live in the Rest of God, I had heard Holy Spirit speak many times that I would learn to fly. His Word clearly says we were all made for flight!

Soar[1] (noun)

- To fly upward; To fly at a great height, without visible movements of the pinions;

- To glide along at a height; To rise or ascend to a height;

- To rise or aspire to a higher or more exalted level.

Stillness[2] (noun)

- The absence of sound or noise: hush, noiselessness, quiet, quietness, silence, soundlessness, still.

- An absence of motion or disturbance: calm, calmness, hush, lull, peace, peacefulness, placidity, placidness, quiet, quietness, serenity, tranquility, untroubledness.

My question posed in the above poem is a real question: How are *stillness* in the Presence of God (where we begin to perceive the magnanimity of His Kingdom) and *soaring* in that magnanimity related? Does one come before the other, or is it a mixture all the way, like the baby bird contemplating, and finally stepping off the edge of the nest before she knows she can actually fly. Does she discover flight in the waiting, or in the moment of finally achieving it?

Invited to flag during music worship with a young friend at her church, I saw the tall perpendicular cloud of the Presence of the Lord come large through the door during prayer beforehand. I heard the Lord say, "Will you receive what I want to bring, that My fullness will fill the temple? Will you receive My stillness?"

I thought the word was for this church since that is who I was praying for, and they are in all ways and expressions passionate for God, and particularly in this season, to enter His new thing. After all, "Can you not perceive it?"[3] was the banner at the front of the church.

My first thought was, "This stillness may be the 'new thing' God has for them, but I don't know if they'll be able to hear it. There's so much noise!" The question and invitation may well have been for them too, but in the days and weeks which followed, Holy Spirit revealed that the word was for me! I thought I carried stillness already. He was showing me there is more. Much MORE!

STILLNESS

Can you hear it?
Can you see it?
Can you perceive it?
Will you BE it?
Still.
Know.
I AM.
The LORD is in His holy temple: Me!
I hush
silent
before Him.

"But the Lord is in his holy temple; let all the earth keep silence before him!"

— HABAKKUK 2:20, NRSV

"But those who wait upon God get fresh strength. They spread their wings and soar like eagles. They run and don't get tired, they walk and don't lag behind."

— ISAIAH 40:31, MSG

Activations For Learning to Be Loved

SOARING AND STILLNESS

Breath of Life ~

"Let Me feed you
Let Me grow you.
I have provision you know nothing of.
Simply trust Me, rest, allow Me to lead.
No fear ever
you are perfectly loved.
Receive stillness – you are My temple! Hush. Allow your
being to be silent, still.
Receive what it is to trust Me, to know Me, for your core
to BE Me.
This is your DNA.
I AM your DNA."

Selah ~

Do you hear the constant invitation, almost a command, to BE
STILL? To listen? To wait? To know? To SOAR?

On That Note ~

Stillness by Klaus (2015 piano solo album)

Pray the Word ~

"You are holy – my holy God, my Father. Thank You that as I am still, silent before You, waiting upon You, that You fill me with fresh strength. You invigorate me to be ready, equipped to SOAR! I receive Your peace, and I believe Your promise. Help me to never leave Your waiting-time ahead of Your leading, that I may receive all You want to give. May I live a constant, waiting-upon-You life, that I am always ready to soar when You say, "Fly!"

45

THE BEDROCK OF FRIENDSHIP

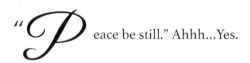 "*P*eace be still." Ahhh...Yes.

Bedrock[1] (noun)

- Solid rock underlying loose deposits such as soil or alluvium;

- The fundamental principles on which something is based.

Way back in the eighties our family would frequently gather with a wonderful group of friends, get out guitars and a banjo, and clap and sing together. It was fun and we laughed a LOT! One of our favourite songs was "Sandy Land," based on Luke 6:47-49:

> *"As for everyone who comes to me and hears my words and puts*
> *them into practice, I will show you what they are like. They are*

like a man building a house, who dug down deep and laid the foundation on rock. When a flood came, the torrent struck that house but could not shake it, because it was well built. But the one who hears my words and does not put them into practice is like a man who built a house on the ground without a foundation. The moment the torrent struck that house, it collapsed and its destruction was complete."

— LUKE 6:47-49, NIV

"No other foundation can be laid except Jesus Christ the Messiah, all built upon Him, whether with gold, silver, precious stones, wood, hay, straw..."

— I CORINTHIANS 3:11-12, ESV

Friendship (noun)

- A person whom one knows well and is fond of; intimate associate; close acquaintance.[2]

- Synonyms: amity, camaraderie, friendliness, comradeship, companionship, fellow feeling, closeness, affinity, rapport, understanding, harmony, unity.[3]

- A state of mutual trust and support.[4]

Sitting with Jesus one day, wondering about all He meant when He called His disciples (and all who followed afterwards) His friends, I heard Him say to me, "You have wanted to walk with Me as Enoch – I am bringing you into My Friendship. You walk with Me well."

*"And Enoch walked (in habitual fellowship – friendship) with God;
and he was not, for God took him (home with Him). [Heb. 11:5.]"*

— GENESIS 5:24, AMPC

*"I do not call you servants (slaves) any longer, for the servant does
not know what his Master is doing (working out). But I have called
you My friends, because I have made known to you everything
that I have heard from My Father. (I have revealed to you everything I learned from Him)."*

— JOHN 15:15, AMPC

I asked Jesus, "How is it that being Your friend seems even
closer than being Your beloved?!! Is it? Or is it simply another
aspect of relationship?"

"Friendship is the Bedrock of relationship," He said, "solid
ground, unchanging, stable. I am inviting you to truly be My
friend.

> 'Tarry ye awhile in this place' beloved.
> Live it Live it Live it
> Receive it Receive it Receive it
> My Friendship will never be snatched away.
> I AM building in you
> deep
> solid
> B e d r o c k."

Think of it – a friend of God. As the definition above says,
friendship is a relationship of camaraderie, fondness, intimacy,
closeness, rapport, harmony, *mutual* trust and support. It seems
beyond comprehension to be that kind of friend with God(!)

except that we've been gradually recognising that we were created to live in close relationship with Him. He delights in us, He loves to be with us, loves to see our face and hear our voice! He loves to walk and talk with us, for us to come to Him with every need, joy, question, and Jesus said it: "I call you my Friend."

Surely this is a profound relationship promotion, the worth and experience of it truly received and cherished. He loves us deep. As Bedrock. Our foundation just got even stronger.

> "For the greatest love of all is a love that sacrifices all. And this great love is demonstrated when a person sacrifices his life for his friends. You show that you are my intimate friends when you obey all that I command you. I have never called you 'servants,' because a master doesn't confide in his servants, and servants don't always understand what the master is doing. But I call you my most intimate friends, for I reveal to you everything that I've heard from my Father."
>
> — JOHN 15:13-15, TPT

> "You are my best friend and my shepherd. I always have more than enough. You offer me a resting place in Your luxurious love. Your tracks take me to an oasis of peace, the quiet brook of bliss. That's where You restore and revive my life. You open before me pathways to God's pleasure and lead me along in Your footsteps of right-eousness so that I can bring honor to Your name. Lord, even when your path takes me through the valley of deepest darkness, fear will never conquer me, for you already have! You remain close to me and lead me through it all the way. Your authority is my strength and my peace. The comfort of your love takes away my fear. I'll never be lonely, for you are near. You become my delicious feast even when my enemies dare to fight. You anoint me with the

fragrance of your Holy Spirit; you give me all I can drink of you until my heart overflows. So why would I fear the future? For your goodness and love pursue me all the days of my life. Then afterward, when my life is through, I'll return to your glorious presence to be forever with you!"

— PSALM 23:1-6, TPT

Activations For Learning to Be Loved

THE BEDROCK OF FRIENDSHIP

Selah ~

What comes to mind and heart as you consider friendship with Jesus? Is it beyond understanding, a heart cry of longing too good or crazy to be true?

Does your heart rise within you to love Him with everything you have and everything you are? Are you willing for the loose and shifting pieces of your life to be built up with gold, silver, and precious stones into something beautiful? What are some of those loose shifting pieces that you would like Him to transform?

Pray the Word ~

"May my life and breath be as precious jewels that reflect Your radiance, as gold purified seven times in the fire, reflecting Your pure goodness and glory. May my life be built upon You, the author and perfector of my faith: may my little loose stones (you can be specific here) be transformed upon Your bedrock to brilliantly reflect Your beauty. Jesus, You have called me Your intimate friend. You invite me to walk with you as Enoch did, to lean in close to hear Your voice as

John the Beloved did. Your Friendship is my Bedrock foundation, my stability, my rest - I am amazed! and humbled. Thank You for revealing Your Father, MY Father, to me, that I may know His nature and live from my true identity - a loved and cared for child and friend of God. Thank You for Your sacrifice on my behalf, that I may be restored to intimate relationship with Him.

Thank You that Your provision covers every need I will ever experience, whether it be peace, food and shelter, safety, restoration, refreshment, guidance, wisdom, deliverance, freedom from fear, profound hope.

You are Holy Holy Holy, and I love You with all my being."

46

FEASTING AND FATNESS!

ave you ever been hungry? I mean really, really hungry? Starving even? Starvation of the physical body is one thing; starvation of the soul, of the heart, is quite another.

Starve[1]

(intransitive verb)

- To perish from lack of food
- To suffer extreme hunger
- (archaic) to die of cold
- (British) to suffer greatly from cold
- To suffer or perish from deprivation (starved for affection)

(transitive verb)

- To kill with hunger
- To deprive of nourishment

- To cause to capitulate by or as if by depriving of nourishment
- To destroy by or cause to suffer from deprivation.

Way back in the beginning in the Garden, Holy God, full of joyful anticipation, created man and woman in His image and in His likeness: brilliant, creative, with authority, wisdom, and joy! He placed them into the abundance of the Garden, a profusion of colourful provision in sights, scents and sounds, and gave them meaningful work and responsibility.

Most of all, He created man and woman to be His friends, to walk and talk with Him and be His family. Sadly, that first man and woman fell victim to deception and made a choice that changed humanity forever. They listened to the deceiving voice of the serpent, that "surely God didn't mean this... Take the fruit..."[2]

They lost their abundance, their hearts, and ours with them. And they began to know what starvation is: desperate hunger for the Presence of the One Who loves, Who devoted Himself to leading His dear ones back to His Feast and gave Himself to be our Food.

Fatness

One day, I heard this:

> "Take My hand – I will lead you.
> May I have this Dance?
> New steps.
> They shall become second nature in a very short time,
> for they are exactly fitted for you. And you shall grow by
> leaps and bounds, full of My fatness – rich, luscious
> taste and fragrance and you shall prepare My food for

My children – choicest of fruits – and they will eat and receive My fatness too...
Your heart is for Me, not yourself, and you are going to be surprised at how much you will receive blessing as you move into the Fullness of My prepared place for you to thrive in.
Receive, My beloved – receive your life.
Dance!"

My heart responded, "I put my hand in Yours! Take me where You want to go. Give me new creative expressions, and deliver me from any conforming, limiting thoughts or old habits. Holy Spirit of Living God, come! Breathe in me, Breath of Heaven. Blow on my garden, cause the seeds You have planted to germinate, send out roots into Your lush soil, and strike out upward to Your Light, that I may be refreshed in Your nutritious food – You – Bread, Wine, and Living Water of Heaven. Feed me, fill me up with Your fatness."

Feast (noun)

- An elaborate and usually abundant meal often accompanied by a ceremony or entertainment: banquet
- Something that gives unusual or abundant enjoyment, a visual feast.
- Abundance, profusion.

Fatness[3]

"Fatness" is used figuratively for the richness of God's goodness; as such it is the translation of deshen ("They shall be abundantly satisfied (margin "Hebrew watered") with the fatness of thy house" (Psalms 36:8; "Thy paths drop fatness" (Psalms 65:11; compare Isaiah 55:2; Jeremiah 31:14).

"You become my delicious feast even when my enemies dare to fight. You anoint me with the fragrance of your Holy Spirit; you give me all I can drink of you until my heart overflows."

— PSALM 23:5, TPT

"Jesus said to them, "I am the bread of life. The one who comes to me will never go hungry, and the one who believes in me will never be thirsty."

— JOHN 6:35, NET

"[She said distinctly] My beloved is mine and I am his! He pastures his flocks among the lilies."

— SONG OF SONGS 2:16, AMPC

Nourishment

Nourish[4] (verb)

- To provide with the food or other substances necessary for growth, health, and good condition.

Prompted to consider by a brief invitation at a women's writing group, the question sits within me, inviting still. What is it to be nourished? What nourishes me? What is necessary for growth, health, and good condition? I can get by with just enough food and water and shelter, but surely *nourish* is much more than just getting by. Surely *nourishment* is filling up, swelling outward, overfull, warm, and bursting with life in every cell of your being!?

I had to ask myself, "What brings me life like that?" I jotted down some thoughts: sunshine, music, quiet, thoughtfulness, being hugged by Salix, starry night sky, forests, rippling brooks and creeks, trees, big trees, mountains, books, lots of books, creativity, choral singing, Italian food, eating in pubs by the fire, walking along the river, sitting down to write, being received... That last is maybe first: being received, welcomed, known – the great hunger of our (or at least *my*) humanity.

Then, I became aware of how inward-focused my first thoughts were. They are real and true and part of my fearfully-and-wonderfully-madeness that He delights in so extravagantly! However, I find that there's more, and it flows easily from how He always, ALWAYS receives me, knows me, cheers me on, and satiates the hunger to be seen. With that there's recognition that I am even more nourished and filled when I dance with Jesus, pray with someone in need, see their need met, see them receive hope and healing, make a meal to share with family, give just the right gift, gather with friends who share a common heart, see people set free, sit with my Abba and be loved and love Him back, bring His love in a bowl of soup or a cookie, care for the sick....

And I remember, Ah! I remember what the Word says about losing what you keep but receiving what you give away.[5] I contemplate the seemingly contradictory promises of God in loving me personally, His tenderness in restoring my soul (my whole being) by quiet waters; His invitation into rest, hiding me in His arms and heart, healing and nourishing all that I am as He affirms my uniqueness. I contemplate His personal care of me with His promise that if I strive to keep my life, I will lose it completely. It will only be in giving it away, in releasing every-thing He has spoken personally into, that I will have true life!

Once again, in His Kingdom there are opposites that are true, and I know that I cannot give up what I do not have. Before I can give my life on the altar, I too need to (get to, am invited to) know what it truly is to be loved, to be whole, to live. When that happens, the giving up of my life that another may experience it will have significance and bear true fruit. When I choose love, rivers of living waters will wash over them as they too step into the realization of being known, that the Most Precious Life was given to save them. And I am nourished to overflowing, happy to be unseen, hidden in the very fullness of His Presence and Glory as He touches the "least of these;" nourishment multiplying outward, Your always-whispers of life. And I give thanks.

"You show me the path of Life; IN YOUR PRESENCE is Fullness of Joy, at Your right hand are pleasures, (life, NOURISHMENT over-flowing, cup running over!), FOREVERMORE."

— PS.16:11, ESV, EMPHASIS AND ADDITION
MINE

"Meanwhile, the disciples urged Him saying, Rabbi, eat something. But He assured them, I have food (nourishment) to eat of which you know nothing and have no idea. So His disciples said one to another, Has someone brought Him something to eat? Jesus said to them, My food (nourishment) is to do the will (pleasure) of Him Who sent Me and to accomplish and completely finish His work."

— JOHN 4:32-24, AMPC

Activations For Learning to Be Loved

FEASTING AND FATNESS!

Breath of Life ~

"I want to take you out of linear thinking and give you the ability to see in new dimensions. You shall fly and you shall know a freedom you have never known before, only tasted beginnings of. I have so much more for you My beautiful treasure – I have life, beauty, peace, and freedom from constraints. Choose trust every moment. Your hiddenness in Me is sacred. I gift you with play, My delightful one: with joy and lightness of being, Full of the fruit from My Tree of Life."

Selah ~

Did you know you are God's beautiful treasure? Are you hungry? Would you like to be fed at His feast, "pastured among the lilies" with Jesus?

On That Note ~

Richard Blanchard. *Fill My Cup*. Warner Chappell Music, Inc., Capitol Christian Music Group, 1959.

Pray the Word ~

"Ah, my Jesus, I am hungry for You, for the rich food of Your Presence. You Who are the bread of heaven, feed me with Yourself and quench my parched being with Your fresh living water. May I always walk with You in the fragrant garden of relationship with You, be fed with Your love."

47

PEACE

*H*oly Spirit of Living God, in His goodness, has whispered and poured out the Peace of our Father frequently within and over me through the years, gifting a shroud of quiet in every cell. Yet, in this last season, peace (true peace of heart, mind, soul, spirit, and body, the peace that is far beyond any understanding,[1] settling all round) has begun to be an important aspect of the foundation and atmosphere of living continually in the One Who *is* peace.[2]

Isaiah, the Old Testament prophet who began his ministry some 740 years before Christ was born, prophesied clearly that there was One coming Who was different, Who would be peace.

> *"For to us a Child is born, to us a Son is given; and the government shall be upon His shoulder, and His name shall be called Wonderful Counselor, Mighty God, Everlasting Father [of Eternity], Prince of Peace."*

> — ISAIAH 9:6, AMPC

From a word study on *shalom*, the Hebrew word for "peace":

> The word translated *peace* in the Old Testament is the Hebrew
> word *shalom*. Our English word *peace* is only one aspect of the
> full meaning of *shalom*. *Shalom* (from salam/salem/shalam),
> means to be safe, sound, healthy, perfect, complete. *Shalom*
> signifies a sense of well-being and harmony both within and
> without – completeness, wholeness, peace, health, welfare,
> safety, soundness, tranquility, prosperity, fullness, rest,
> harmony; the absence of agitation or discord, a state of calm
> without anxiety or stress.[3]

The root meaning of *shalom* is to be whole or sound, and this
leads to translations that speak of completeness, wholeness,
well-being, welfare, and peace. *Shalom* also includes the idea of
vigour and vitality in all dimensions of life. In short, *shalom*
speaks of holistic ("holy") health for our souls and spirits.

Reading the promises of God with *shalom* in mind expands our
understanding of His tender, loving, fully accessible heart
for us!

> *"The Lord spoke to Moses, saying, "Speak to Aaron and his sons,*
> *saying, Thus you shall bless the people of Israel: you shall say to*
> *them, The Lord bless you and keep you; the Lord make his face to*
> *shine upon you and be gracious to you; the Lord lift up his counte-*
> *nance upon you and give you peace (shalom)."*

— NUMBERS 6:24-26, ESV, AMPLIFICATION
ADDED

The above passage could read like this:

The Lord told Moses to tell all the people: I the Lord commit to care for you as a good father with his children, to guard and protect you in every way. My face is always shining toward you, all My love and fellowship is always for you; I look upon you constantly, I give you all My Kingdom provision, all of Myself; My Shalom, every good thing, is yours.

In the New Testament, originally written in Greek, the word used to denote "peace" was *eirene*, meaning to join or bind together that which has been separated, the opposite of division or dissension, a state of concord and harmony. *Eirene* can convey the sense of an inner rest, well-being, and harmony.[4]

As we read the following verses, keeping in mind the extended meanings of the Hebrew *shalom* from the Old Testament and the Greek *eirene* from the New Testament (all meant to be encapsulated in the English word, *peace*), how may your heart understanding be enlarged of all Jesus brings – of wholeness, harmony, well-being, tranquility, prosperity, calm, vigor and vitality?

Jesus said:

> "Peace (eirene, shalom) I leave with you; my peace (eirene, shalom) I give to you. Not as the world gives do I give to you. Let not your hearts be troubled, neither let them be afraid. I have said this to you, that in me you may have peace (eirene, shalom). In the world you have tribulation; but be of good cheer, I have overcome the world!"

> — JOHN 14:27; 16:33, RSV, EMPHASIS ADDED

> "Have no anxiety about anything, but in everything by prayer and supplication with thanksgiving let your requests be made known to God. And the peace (eirene, shalom) of God, which passes, tran-

scends, all understanding, will keep, guard, your hearts and your minds in Christ Jesus."

— PHILIPPIANS 4:7, RSV, NIV

Jesus received is 'the Peace that passes understanding,'
the promised,
desired-to-be-gifted
Shalom
of Almighty God.
He is Emmanuel – God with us.

Activations For Learning to Be Loved

PEACE

Selah ~

Are you craving peace? Longing for well-being? Have you asked Jesus to be calm within you? Have you found yourself stuck in a cycle of asking, receiving, losing, asking, and receiving again? His tranquil, vital peace-presence is a daily offering, a daily bread. His supply is endless. Is it time once again to just sit, soak Him in again?

On That Note ~

The Blessing with Kari Jobe and Cody Carnes, Live from Elevation Ballantyne

Pray the Word ~

"Thank You Jesus that You are peace, and that You offer Yourself to me and to all, always. Help me to remember that, just like eating three meals a day (plus snacks!), I need to feed on You frequently and

receive from You regularly, even before the hunger arises! Thank You that Your peace-Presence is far greater than any disturbance or trouble in the world, for You overcame all at Your cross and resurrection. Your victory is complete."

48

JOY

$\mathcal{M}$any years ago I came across this word/promise of God:

"Weeping may endure for a night, but joy comes in the morning."

— PSALM 30:5, AMPC

Joy Comes in the Morning

I have had a LOT of weeping. I have also had many experiences of coming through weeping into joy, building layer upon layer of the truth of the trustworthiness, the faithfulness, and the goodness of God. I have experienced His delight and determination to bring me through difficult burdensome mourning into joy.

Joy[1] (noun)

- The emotion of great delight or happiness caused by something exceptionally good or satisfying; keen pleasure; elation: She felt the joy of seeing her son's success.

- A source or cause of keen pleasure or delight;
- Something or someone greatly valued or appreciated: Her prose style is a pure joy.
- The expression or display of glad feeling; festive gaiety.

I've long known I was called into joy. I thought I knew what joy was, for I've experienced much joy and know I have great capacity for it! But this most recent receiving and entering more deeply into joy is different. It is solid, like bedrock—grounded, firm, unchanging, not to be taken away; It is quiet and deep because joy is not an "it," not an emotion or expression. Jesus in me (one of the fruits of His Spirit Presence living within me) *is* jubilant Joy.[2]

In a "Quote of the Day," Graham Cooke wrote:

> Joy is always on the agenda because joy is the nature of God and it's the abiding atmosphere of heaven. When you die, God isn't going to say, "Well, come in. You did the best you could. Enter in to the misery of your God." No way. JOY is who He is! (emphasis mine)[3]

Joy, true joy, unshakeable, not-determined-by-circumstance-joy, is the very essence of Who Jesus is, always![4] And He and I are one. As the song Amazing Grace sings, "Through many dangers, toils and snares I have already come ... 'tis grace that leads me home."

Your Word is true:
Weeping endures for the night,
and sometimes
the night seems r e a l l y, r e a l l y, l o n g ...

but joy does indeed,
finally,
come in the morning
dawning the new unchangeable day!

"...how blessed all those in whom you live, whose lives become roads you travel; They wind through lonesome valleys, come upon brooks, discover cool springs and pools brimming with rain! God-traveled, these roads curve up the mountain, and at the last turn— Zion! God in full view!"

— PSALM 84:5-7, MSG

Always!

Thank You for being my Shepherd,
my Road,
my Way,
Redeeming ALL,
my Hope, my Stay,
my Peace, the
Cherisher of my heart,
my Righteousness,
Fragrance,
Strong rampart;
Thirst Quencher,
Defender,
Comforter,
Friend ~
Bridegroom,
rich Feast
Joy without end!

Always together,

my heart's greatest treasure,
Loving forever
and EVER,
Amen!

Thank You, Lord, for travelling the road of my life...and inviting me to travel Yours. In the words of the Canadian Army recruitment poster: There's no Life like it!

"He reached down from on high and took hold of me; He drew me out of deep waters. He rescued me from my powerful enemy, from my foes who were too strong for me. They confronted me in the day of my disaster, but the LORD was my support. He brought me out into a spacious place; He rescued me because He delighted in me. ... You, O LORD, keep my lamp burning; my God turns my darkness into light. ... As for God, His way is perfect, the word of the LORD is flawless. He is a shield for all who take refuge in Him."

— PSALM 18:16-19, 28, AND 30, NIV

"I have told you these things, that My joy and delight may be in you, and that your joy and gladness may be of full measure and complete and overflowing."

— JOHN 15:11, AMPC

"... In Your presence is fullness of joy; In Your right hand there are pleasures forever!"

— PSALM 16:11, NASB

"Blessed are those whose strength is in you, whose hearts are set on pilgrimage. As they pass through the Valley of Baka, they make it a place of springs; the autumn rains also cover it with pools. They go from strength to strength, till each appears before God in Zion."

— PSALM 84:5-7, NIV

Activations For Learning to Be Loved

JOY

Selah ~

Where are you on your pilgrimage to the holiness and joy of God? Have you begun? Have you seen Him along the way or has His presence been indistinct, as when He walked (unrecognised) with the two on the Emmaus Road after His resurrection?[5]

May you see Him as He is, where He is, right where you are.

On That Note ~

Reckless Love by Cory Asbury/Bethel Music

Pray the Word ~

"Jesus, thank You for inviting me to journey with You, promising that You are always present, though perhaps not always seen or recognised. Thank You that You draw me out of the miry pit of despair, out of discouragement, out of darkness, to a wide, solid, spacious place

where I can stand and live in You. Thank You for Your intention for all my life to be full of joy! Because of You – because You are bigger than any difficulty – You have conquered every trouble already. Thank You that our Father always has good plans, for delighting in me and bringing me along the way of pilgrimage to Your most holy sanctuary: Your victorious, kind, powerful, full-of-joy heart. Thank You that rest, trust, and joy are where Your roadmap leads, and if (when!) I lose my way from time to time, You always guide me back home."

— Part IX —

SITTING with TRINITY

"Look! Listen! There's my lover! Do you see him coming?
Vaulting the mountains, leaping the hills.
My lover is like a gazelle, graceful; like a young stag, virile.
Look at him there, on tiptoe at the gate,
all ears, all eyes—ready! My lover has arrived and he's
speaking to me! Get up, my dear friend, fair and beautiful
lover—come to me! Look around you: Winter is over; the
winter rains are over, gone! Spring flowers are in blossom all
over. The whole world's a choir—and singing! Spring
warblers are filling the forest with sweet arpeggios. Lilacs are
exuberantly purple and perfumed,
and cherry trees fragrant with blossoms.
Oh, get up, dear friend,
my fair and beautiful lover—come to me!"
Song of Songs 2:8-13, MSG

49

COME UP HERE

$\mathcal{I}$ 've often seen Jesus leaning down towards me from up above on a stairway, with a door opening off to the left into what I know is glory. The light pouring out of that doorway is brilliant and I hear Him say, "Come up here," and He leans forward to take my hand. I've heard Him whisper that a lot: "Come up here." I hear His invitation every time I see craggy, interesting steps, sometimes simple plain stairs...

He's taken me through that door many times.

I remember the first time I looked in from the doorway and saw my Abba, Father God, a ways off in the distance on the Throne of Heaven, with all the angels and archangels and elders and seraphim and cherubim singing and worshipping, and it was GLORIOUS. He was GLORIOUS! He beckoned to me to come near, and though I'd started out as my adult self, when I crossed the golden floors of Heaven, I became smaller and smaller, younger and younger, until I was just my small, quiet-little-girl self, and Abba God, King of Heaven, got down off His throne and sat on the floor with me.

We played tiddly-winks!

He never took His eyes off me. He was never distracted, never checked His watch, never let me know He had a gazillion and one trillion things to do in the world. His eyes just looked at me, completely loving every speck, drinking me in, every cell of me. He ate up every little movement and loved me.

Purely Loved

Abba loved being with me, playing with me, listening to me, and encouraging me. He loved the sound of my voice. He laughed and laughed with me, hung on my words, clapped and applauded. Angels did not try to get His attention for more pressing matters – the time (all the time, always) was just for us.

And I was quiet inside, so quietly safe, with no thought of trying to figure out what He needed me to do to make anything okay, to let Him go back to what He needed to do. I didn't have to do anything but BE. And it was so ... good. Restful. Quiet. Lung-filling, life-giving.

Without being aware of it, I was simply WELL, from the inside out: *loved purely.*

INTO YOUR HEART

Sitting with You once (I'd come with tears),
Your very heart suddenly opened up
took me in,
enveloping,
the moist soft pinkish flesh of Your heart
sealing closed behind my entry –
held
quiet

safe
well.
Reminded me of the time Your Spirit took outlined
     facial form,
swooping from several rows ahead and
came, and
gave me a kiss on my left cheek –
I felt it!
Engulfed in home now,
Wrapped in Your heart now
(and Your smile),
Never lost again –
I know who, and Whose, I am.

"In that day you will know that I am in my Father, and you in me,
and I in you."

— JOHN 14:20, ESV

INTERCESSION 101: A NEW PERSPECTIVE

My Dad ~
... coming to You, looking forward
to see You leave Your throne to
come sit with me on the floor (like last time ...)
but You say
"Come up here"
and pat Your lap as you sit
on the throne of heaven
Of course!
that's what it's all about!
"Come up here"

And I get to snuggle in to You
as You look out over Your vast Kingdom
seeing everything, in charge of everything,
responding, directing, loving, saving
everything
And yet
at the very same time
with not one iota of separation
or distractedness
You hold, and love,
me
And it is so EASY   EASE – Y
natural
unforced
I don't need to be care-full
for anything
So comfortable,
I show You my treasures,
tell You about an injustice & how it made
     me feel
(bad! angry! frustrated! ... not recognising the
     clashing of Kingdoms)
and You smile
snug me tighter
"I've taken care of that" You say.
in a flash I see my Jesus
Your Jesus ... Yourself? ...
on the Cross, against a stormy sky
Blood in thin streams sliding down down
and a waterfall of Life Water
crashing down, deep, clear, refreshing ~
washing washing washing
no grit can stay anywhere
and from my snuggled place on Your lap

just in the flow of our quiet talking, bursts of
    laughter,
You look out over Your vast everything again, quietly
    smiling:
"All this is yours, princess"
I cosy into You
and show You my little dolls,
chattering away
Your smile, Your snug hug, Your rest ~
I never have to leave!
One little, HUGE word from my baby mouth
fells all the giants "out there"
Jesus
JESUS
and terrors topple.
Your rest, Your comfort, Your ease, Your love
never hiccups, glitches,
or even briefly pauses
as I consider (do I consider?) the responsibility, the
    inheritance of
"All this is yours"
I hardly take note ~
well, and held,
in You.
"Let's go eat turkey!
play outside
wash the dishes
set captives free
go for a drive
do the laundry
open the eyes of the blind
sit in the sun
destroy principalities
dance..."

*"The Lord said to Moses, "**Come up** to me on the mountain and stay **here**, and I will give you the tablets of stone with the law and commandments I have written for their instruction."*

— EXODUS 24:12, NIV, EMPHASIS ADDED

*"After this I looked, and there before me was a door standing open in heaven. And the voice I had first heard speaking to me like a trumpet said, "**Come up here**, and I will show you what must take place after this.""*

— REVELATION 4:1, NIV, EMPHASIS ADDED

*"Then they heard a loud voice from heaven saying to them, "**Come up here.**" And they went **up** to heaven in a cloud, while their enemies looked on."*

— REVELATION 11:12, NIV, EMPHASIS ADDED

Activations For Learning to Be Loved

COME UP HERE

Selah ~

Have you heard the invitation of Jesus to "Come up here"? Would you like to? Could it be released from the desire to see, to know, to be engulfed in the presence of the One Who is always reaching out, waiting to speak with you, to show you His treasures, offering His love?

Breath of Life ~

"...Let My quiet be with you.
Learn to let it be okay to not have your ears and eyes
filled up with sounds or scenes or directions.
I am always with you and sometimes it is just for us to
sit on the shore together in quiet, not thinking of what is
coming next and how to prepare, but simply enjoying
the NOW, the Nowhere of NOW HERE (as Brennan
Manning spoke to in Ruthless Trust). This is more
striving falling away, more "must" and "wish" and small
regrets – let them all fall away.

Let Me be the determiner of fruitful time spent,
and you shall learn stillness and freedom from pressure
to move, and to make something happen when My
response seems overlong in coming.

Simply Be.
Held in Me."

Pray the Word ~

"O, my Father, my Redeemer, my Friend – You invite me to be Your sanctuary! Throughout all of Scripture You have invited Your people to be in Your presence, to "Come up Here;" high and lifted up, to see and live from Your perspective, to learn what Your love looks like, even while our enemies look on. You called Moses to "Come up Here" and gave him the tablets of stone, that your people would hear Your instructions for life. You invited John the Beloved to "Come up Here," that he may see what would take place in the future. May I be ready always to hear Your invitation to "Come up Here," that I may receive what You want to give to and through me."

50

ENTOURAGE

*E*ntourage – I Have One!! Entourage comes from the French word *entourer*, meaning "to surround," and means "the people who surround someone," the group of people who travel with and work for an important or famous person.

My ENTOURAGE!

- I AM with you always!

- I will never leave you or forsake you, I will be with you wherever you go!

- Jesus answered, If a person (really) loves Me, he will keep My word; and My Father will love him, and We will come to him and make our home (abode, special dwelling place) with him.

- I will ask the Father and He will give you.... The Spirit of Truth, Whom the world cannot receive (welcome, take into its heart), because it does not see Him or know and recognise Him. But you know and recognise Him, for He lives with you (constantly) and will be in you.

- As the mountains surround Jerusalem, so the Lord is round about His people ...

- The Angel of the LORD encamps round about me to deliver me!

- For He will give His angels (especial) charge over you to accompany and defend and preserve you in all your ways ...

- I'm surrounded by a GREAT CLOUD OF WITNESSES cheering me on! With a company (even a BATTALION, He whispered) of angels.

To have such an esteemed entourage everywhere I go—my Father, my Saviour Friend, my Counsellor, Comforter, Anointer, Teacher, life's breath, angels (battalions of angels!), a great cloud of witnesses, all the host of heaven—I must be pretty important!

Dear one, you are too.

Easter 2017

I had been anticipating this day – Easter Sunday – for quite some time. Not because it is any different from any other day, because Jesus is alive always and has been since that first Easter morning, and for sure I don't just celebrate His risen life just once a year!

But today, this once-a-year day, is a day that is recognised all around the world and has been a day of celebration all around the world for the past 1,985 years or so! And, being one who loves to worship the One Who loves me, who loves to dance with Him and sing, to live with joy, I had anticipated doing all that (and more) on this day especially.

I planned to post the YouTube link to Kari Jobe's incredible song *Forever* and let it speak for itself. I planned to put on Handel's Messiah, which I've always felt it is more fitting for the Easter season, rather than Christmas. I planned to fill my home with music and colour and dance before the Throne of the Living God with all the cherubim and seraphim, the elders and the angels and all the living creatures shouting Hosanna! Holy, Holy, Holy! Blessing and Honour and Glory and Power be unto the Lamb Who was slain, Who has begun His reign!

I LOVE to dance!

Not being part of a church that was meeting this weekend, (we meet in lots of other times and ways and places), and knowing there are all manner of incredible life-filled gatherings of celebrators today that we could join with, I still heard the invitation to simply meet with Him here, in His quiet Presence.

All through the weekend, beginning on (Good) Friday, His Spirit whispered of what He did for love: six hours of incredible torture (not to mention all that led up to that), hanging, nailed through His hands and feet on a cross of wood, every single organ having life squeezed out ever so slowly, one cell at a time; pure excruciating agony.

He did it for love.

He did it to clear the way for me, for you! Not to save us from an angry punishing God who needed placating, but to invite us back into relationship with His Father Who loves, invited back to wholeness, to life, to silence all the noisy accusing condemning voices, to demolish all fear, to capture and redeem every tear, to restore hope, to pour out joy, that we may truly live in peace!

I've seen His eyes, many times, as He is hanging on the Cross, piercing right into mine. They are laser-like, intense, yet so full of love and tenderness. They know every part of me, all the worst hidden parts too, yet are full of compassion and love, as He weeps for me, for my freedom.

"I did it for LOVE!" He says.

And on this anticipated day of extra-fueled celebration for His bursting out of that tomb and turning the world upside down forevermore, on this day of thanksgiving and praise, this April 16, 2017, I found only quiet within me.

Awe.

Stillness.

Nothing is worthy enough to celebrate Him with: no music, no dance, no word – not right now at least. Only silence. Hidden in His heart. Home.

I See You (1)

Bleary with sleep, making coffee, I look over and
there You are
sitting at my table
waiting ... for me!
smiling

Walking, pondering heavily along the darkened path,
*   I look up and*
there You are
brilliant
dazzling
behind the clouds

Sleep not coming easy, brain a jumble, ready to give
*   up, I open my eyes and*
there You are
sitting right beside me
present
still

Playing my piano, halting, mistake ridden, I look to
*   my left and*
there You are
enjoying
clapping
for joy!

Serious, figuring, frowning, determining, I look
*   out and*
there You are
in the River
laughing
beckoning me,
"C'mon in, the water's FINE!"

"I know you
I am always with you
I Am your helper
I will never leave you
I go before you, preparing your way

I AM your healer
I AM your peace
My joy is for you

Come away My beloved, My fair one ~
Come and Dance in the River
Here I AM!"

I SEE YOU (2)

Considering the weighty needs of the world, feeling
grieved, discouraged, I look further and
there You are
bringing cups of cold water, food, medicine, commu-
nity, hope
sharing forgiveness, love, healing, skills, mercy,
support
through presence, painting, dancing, music, teaching,
serving, studying, creating, building, digging
holes, planting gardens, helping neighbours,
fighting oppression, listening, noticing, work and
play, laughter and shared tears ... so much more
...
I see an army of You
tender
fierce
courageous
unflinching
"I bring Light into the darkness
I bring freedom to those in captivity
I give sight to the blind!

I make wars cease, breaking the bow & shattering
    the spear,
returning good for evil, Love for hate
I Love you and will love through you
as you reflect My smile, My dazzling brilliance, My
    patience, My joy
for as much as you do to the least, you do to Me;
Where you are,
I AM!"[1]

I See You, Feel You, Hear You, Sense You, Taste You (3)

In my daughter and son-in-law loving their son
in my grandson's purity, focus, innocence
in the powerful mountains and
the meal shared with friends, in the
sun suddenly appearing, blazing, PRESENT; in
wafting fragrance from flowers, bread baking, garlic
    & onions frying in butter
in fresh breeze off the water,
birds twittering, rabbits and gophers bounding;
roaring of lions, ribbitting frogs,
songs of whales,
waving blades of grass, fields of wheat, quiet forests,
    chattering chipmunks
a single teardrop, a thankful smile;
in compassion, colours, exotic flavours, emotions,
    passion, pardon
in fury at injustice
in the choice to trust Light though all appears black
in laughter, in stillness, in cacophony of celebratory joy

in varying gifts and skills, our brain! our bodies! vast
variety of animals, plants, humanity!
in music, in harmony, in disparity, in questions,
in the quest for Your More
in contentment with what is

"I AM the Bread of life, I AM Christ through all in all
above all, every good and perfect gift is from Me
with Whom there is no variation or shadow due
to change – I AM Christ the same yesterday,
today, forever – LIFE!
Everything was made through Me and nothing that
is was made without Me – all, ALL, carries My
stamp, My essence, My heart.
I created you to know Me.
I gave you My creation to know the boundless
creativity of My love.
I give you Myself, that you may receive all."²

I see You everywhere I look
I hear You when I do not see
I sense You when I do not hear
I know You when I do not sense
You still Are when I do not know
for You ARE I AM.

OUT OF THE CAGE

You've said I'll be an eagle
with the heart of a dove,
flying high and seeing,
releasing Your love...

I only want to see You,

that when you look at me
adoration, thanks and laughter
are all that YOU see!

Like a favourite old sweater
or aged slippers, just right,
our consanguinity sustains me,
fits me well for new heights...

Knowing I can trust You,
my wings lifted on Your Wind,
new vistas open widely
through You, my trusted Friend.

O powerful most Holy,
High God You ARE —
You found me, the wee-est
searched me out, take me far.

Now my tears are not from sorrow,
they're birthed in grateful awe;
I am the dancing one before You
Holy Trinity,
- Brilliant, Glorious, Incredible, Awesome, Just,
Redeeming, Inspiring, Healing,
Kind -
Loving God.

(You don't fit within any rules, walls or boxes ...
and now I don't have to either)

How I love You!

<u>Words</u>

There are all kinds of Words –

Life words, death words, vibrant words, stolen words,
* sarcastic words, true and false words.*
You appear to think quite highly of words
of course, You know their power – You, the Word at
* the beginning, if*
beginning can be used for something someOne never
* begun, always IS, (I AM!) ever onward;*
Creative Word, Your very nature bursting in every
* cell of Life,*
Nothing seen or unseen without Your declaration:

BE!

Your gifts through words affirm, heal, reveal, leading,
* teaching, ever reaching into our deepest selves,*
* heart's shelves laden oft with longing, wanting*
* higher, more*
than we are just yet,
drawing further into sight, You apprise just right the
shutters of our
heart eyes.

Simon P. spoke all negating, truly stating: who else is
* there to go to? None has Life words except You*
* Who ARE Life Word, no strife,*
Your knife of word deboning, cleanly honing false
* enthroning till all that's left*
is pure.

Simple really, clearly, cleanly, keenly offering

Hope, responding lives give up demise
for vivid Joy!

You caution: "Watch your words" – their power so
        mighty, destroying, much deployed
by one loose lip, one tiny slip of tongue to
offend, to bend, deny a friend, oppress one weaker
than we, sharing stories best kept silent, caustic wit
        destruction upon
vulnerable soul once whole til we slice & dice, putre-
        fying the air with the pit's
vile ugly, calling it joking ... or the evolution of
        language,
haha
But You said, showed, led, that what is spoken bears
        fruit – for life or death, we choose, we lose
or win
BIGTIME
through our tamed, or not, tongue's fire -
word choice.

Inviting Your lovers to seasoned-with-salt Grace, ears
        keeping pace with heaven's
embrace, tantalised, brought alive, not despised, no
        demising,
birthing more galore than ever before
of Life, no
dullness, only transporting, vibrant cavorting to
        vocal cords chortling with their purpose for
        being!
How vile the thief oppressor, distorting Your Life
        words by determined abuse,
accusation, obtuse, not revelation, of
Your heart of Love

but of hate, condemnation, punishing justification of
evil schemes in Your 'name', falsely claimed to be
true, to be You,
but are not.
Stolen receptors cannot receive when Word of Life is
used as
a bullet in the heart.

O God O God I cry for lives impacted, those who've
had Your Life word
redacted, becoming rules or torturous lies;
expose the liar using words to thrill, chill, kill, leaving
nil but empty
death. You Who ARE Word meet those needing,
bleeding ones,
not resistant just unable to receive Your Word as
spoken, only broken, give some token in other
signs of Love ... bring sunsets,
sunrises, fill the skies with
whispering You
in ways that can be received.

Glorious Word be seen
in every language every place that all may taste
unending Grace, Your Goodness wide high, to the sky.
and beyond;
Come Word in all Your Glory, tell your Story, bring
Your More; that hearts awaken
where we're shaken, to what we've always hoped,
needed, known
was here, there, everywhere:
You!
True

HOW MUCH DID IT HURT?

I once asked You how it felt to create the world... You
said You had fun!
that You loved everything You did,
that it was all soooo good!! And Your face was
shining with Joy!

How much did it hurt You then,
to send them from the Garden?
What were Your tears at the loss of Your talks?
You formed them
from dust and rib,
Breathed in Your own Life,
Taught and gave ALL You had made
into their hands.

You Loved!! Delighted!!
Enjoyed walks in the cool of the day ...
til they believed a snake,
and doubted You.

You Who are Beauty, Kindness itself,
Love larger than imagining,
w i d e r than G a l a x i e s;
and they broke with you,
for an apple.
How much did it hurt You
to send them away, letting them see
there are consequences to choice,
The stain of agreeing with the liar,
the tempter,
the mocking serpent,

simply not able to stay in the presence of Your own
    Pure Holiness,
the yeast of despising rooted,
sprouting its fruit already
in the hiding - the death
You never wanted them to experience.

How much did it hurt You
to see them struggle and fight,
kill each other, believe lies,
fall sick, destroy ...
only a tiny filament of faith from
Your heart to ears even yet soft to Your Voice
running through all the clans of man,
sheep, for the most part, caught up in their own ruts,
    fears and filth,
following other shepherds...
O how Your heart must have hurt ...
must STILL hurt,
at all the greed, all the hatred
all the despisings, disregard,
all the lies and misconstructions,
cancer-spreading desecrations of
ALL You declared and meant for GOOD.

And still do.

That's the thing, isn't it?
You still see who and what You created – before the
    blight came in
and twisted
 pouring putrid pestilence into hearts,
destroying lives from A to Z.
You still see the Good,

the Gem
underneath.

And You keep loving, inviting, calling,
"Come!
Come!! Come Through the Blood Bath of My Son
Who paid your debt of separation, took all the
    muddy filth into Himself
that you may be CLEAN,
delivered,
Restored to My Garden of extravagant Abundance;
Come back
to Me!"

O Father – You must be pretty strong
to withstand the excruciating pain of all Your kids
who still don't want anything
to do with You.

I guess it's not unusual
that I would sometimes share Your pain then...
since we share a Heart

Activations For Learning to Be Loved

ENTOURAGE

Selah ~

Are you aware of all that great cloud of witnesses that are cheering you on, of the angelic host assigned to guard you, of Trinity God surrounding, living within you? Do you know the powerful impact of every word you utter? Have you begun to see God revealing Himself in multitudinous places? Have you considered the depth and breadth of the Kingdom of God, His profound heart of Love for you, for ALL the world, every single person in it? When was the last time you spent time looking at the Cross of Jesus and what was won there for you?

———

On That Note ~

When I Look at the Blood by Godfrey Birtell

———

Pray the Word ~

My prayer for all who are in MY heart, from Ephesians chapter 3, verses 14-19, 20-21 in the Message Translation:

"My response is to get down on my knees before the Father, this magnificent Father who parcels out all heaven and earth. I ask him to strengthen you by his Spirit—not a brute strength but a glorious inner strength —that Christ will live in you as you open the door and invite him in. And I ask him that with both feet planted firmly on love, you'll be able to take in with all followers of Jesus the extravagant dimensions of Christ's love. Reach out and experience the breadth! Test its length! Plumb the depths! Rise to the heights! Live full lives, full in the fullness of God. God can do anything, you know —far more than you could ever imagine or guess or request in your wildest dreams! He does it not by pushing us around but by working within us, his Spirit deeply and gently within us.

> *Glory to God in the church!*
> *Glory to God in the Messiah, in Jesus!*
> *Glory down all the generations!*
> *Glory through all millennia! Oh, yes!"*

51

INVITATION TO THE RIVER

On Saturday, July 11, 2015, while soaking to "Dancing River" by Alberto Rivera & Friends, I had a vision:

I am back a ways, by the tree line, a bit of a hard dirt/grass packed clearing in front of me, facing a clear flowing river, rather like the size of the Bow River at Edworthy Park, Calgary. On the other side of the river are thick evergreen trees going up a high hill, lush and green. Above is brilliant blue summer sky.

I see Jesus standing in the middle of the river. He's looking at me with a huge grin on His face and beckons me to come – come to Him in the river.

I do!

I slip off my shoes and run into the river with Him and we splash and play, dive under water and hold our breath, swim, come up laughing, jump up and down holding onto each other's arms, float on our backs looking up at the sky – at the blue and the clouds and the pigeons and the eagles high above. The air is fresh, warm, and all kinds of birds are singing and calling, chattering in the evergreens beside us.

Then He takes my hand and soars up into the sky, up high with the eagles, soaring round and round and up and up, silhouetted against the sun, over the other side of the river, then back over to the side I was on at the beginning, flying above and then lower, through the trees – I saw a white owl on a branch look at me as we went past! but we keep on going, Jesus just holding my hand, me flying along behind Him, full of freedom, ease, refreshment, joy – more alive and loved than ever before!

We fly back to the river – only now there is our Catch The Fire (CTF) Calgary Family, laughing and playing and splashing with Jesus and each other – a hoot! Floating, being loved, free, pulling pranks under water, no one left out, no one more special, everyone the same – incredible enjoyment!

And then He takes someone's hand, and we all take the hand of someone near us, and we soar in a flowing line up, up, up into the sky, among the birds, the eagles, against the sun, over the trees, and He takes us further than before, to the edge of the atmosphere of the earth (I see the globe!). We are full of laughter and joy, with Him, in His presence, free, flying, flying!

It becomes evening, and we are on the near side of the river around a campfire, roasting marshmallows, visiting in comfortable little quiet groups; no competition, no one left out, Jesus' face lit up by the light of the fire, full of rest and love, storytelling. There are small tents around the perimeter of the fire, each with a lantern glowing within. In a while it comes time to go to bed (for He gives to His beloved sleep!), and we each go to our own tent, blowing out our lanterns, laying our heads down upon our pillows, resting so comfortably, a smile on each face.

I 'see' the Spirit begin to whisper into each one sleeping, and we each begin to dream the same dream: we see Jesus on the river on a very large catamaran – a party boat! He is grinning ear to ear and beckoning us to come to Him in the river and play and see and fly with Him... So, we do! laughter! music!

After a time, I see each of us in many different places and lives, and I see each of us in ones and twos, sitting with or walking alongside of all kinds of different people in all manner of walks of life – teachers, doctors, garbage collectors, secretaries, students in classrooms, scientists, computer geeks, children and many more. Each one is being met individually in their places of life, being loved, walked with, becoming known, and eventually being given invitation to come to the river. Some are hidden way back in dark caves of despair, being drawn out slowly, hands held lovingly, drawn into the light and invited to the river.

And all those invited are with us, joined together in great joy, with Jesus in the river – laughing, playing, splashing, welcoming, enjoying — no one was left out, tons of exuberant freedom!

Then the flying begins again – Jesus takes a hand and we all take the hand of someone next to us and He flies up into the sky, soaring, soaring, silhouetted against the sun, and He takes us beyond the earth, up into the outer atmosphere, and I see the Father huge against the starry galaxy, playing a violin over the earth – I could see His music, the notes of His song playing over us and all His loved creation as Jesus soars and gives life with thousands flowing behind Him, spinning circles throughout space, other planets, and the sun in near or far or wide proximity.

We fly back to earth, each to further away places. We are taken to east Asia, and to tiny little dark places where multitudes are in terrible darkness, eyes black, devoid of life, and we individually meet up with ones and twos and love them, quietly bringing joy, inviting to the river, where we all meet together again and again and again and again, only more and more, more and more life, more joy, more and more freedom.

And on it goes

Flying

Soaring

Freedom

LIFE

Joy!

> "Jesus replied, "If you only knew who I am and the gift that God wants to give you—you'd ask me for a drink, and I would give to you living water."
>
> — JOHN 4:10, TPT

> "Jesus said, "...Anyone who drinks the water I give will never thirst —not ever. The water I give will be an artesian spring within, gushing fountains of endless life."
>
> — JOHN 4:14, MSG

> "He who believes in Me [who cleaves to and trusts in and relies on Me] as the Scripture has said, From his innermost being shall flow [continuously] springs and rivers of living water."
>
> — JOHN 7:38, AMPC

> "Then the angel showed me the river of the water of life, flowing with water clear as crystal, continuously pouring out from the throne of God and of the Lamb. The river was flowing in the

middle of the street of the city, and on either side of the river was the Tree of Life, with its twelve kinds of ripe fruit according to each month of the year. The leaves of the Tree of Life are for the healing of the nations. "It is my gift to you! Come."

— REVELATIONS 22:1-2; 17, TPT

Activations For Learning to Be Loved

INVITATION TO THE RIVER

Selah ~

Have you heard the invitation to the River of God that flows from His Throne? Are you still on the banks looking on? Have you begun to dip your toes in? Have you jumped in with a big SPLASH?! What part of the Invitation to the River vision speaks to you?

On That Note ~

Deep Cries Out by William Matthews/Christiann Koepke/Bethel Music

---

Pray the Word ~

"Jesus, how is it that when I look at You, I see Your face of Joy for me alone. Then You widen the awareness, and it includes everyone – loved individually — and the Joy is exponentially, thrillingly MORE. Your heart's desire for every hidden, hurting one to be restored to Life

is constant. Show me where I fit as one of Your River-full-of-Life Joy bringers. May I always meet others with Your tender heart, drawing each one as You lead, into Your River of Life."

52

HIGHER

I saw You, Jesus, slightly above me, a little to the right, a grin of eagerness on Your face, eyes smiling, full of Love, and something more... Anticipation? Incredible Joy?!

Higher[1] (adjective)

- When something is described as higher, it's more advanced, difficult, or complex. Higher education is what you learn in college or graduate school, and it's more complicated than high school. You're most likely to see the adjective higher being used to specify a type of education or schooling.

Reaching out Your arm toward me, I hear:

"Come with Me,
My sweet flying Pea,
Take My hand – we're going higher..."

<u>AND!</u>

"Take My hand – we're going higher ~"
And I do!
excited for seeing, living MORE ~
More fully alive,
even More closely in awareness of Your Presence,
anticipating MORE, greater revelations of Heaven!
... And then remembering that to go higher
means to go lower,
as You did...
Servant of all.
Death in exchange for Life.
And I thought of maturity.
No more handheld bottles of milk.
Solid food.
And I knew where I would
'see You most clearly,
be with You most dearly'
as Richard, Bishop of Chichester asked for
way back on April 3, 1253:
With the long neglected,
lonely forgotten ones,
the bruised and wounded ones,
the ones needing
a Friend.
Every word AND story You gave
was followed by Your "in addition to,"
Your
And:
invitation into Your very Presence—

*"...I was hungry **and** you gave me food, I was thirsty **and** you gave me drink, I was a stranger **and** you welcomed me, I was naked **and** you clothed me, I was sick **and** you visited me, I was in prison **and** you came to me." Then the righteous will answer him, saying,*

"Lord, when did we see you hungry and feed you, or thirsty and give you drink? And when did we see you a stranger and welcome you, or naked and clothe you? And when did we see you sick or in prison and visit you?" And the King will answer them, "Truly, I say to you, as you did it to one of the least of these my brothers, you did it to me."

— MATTHEW 25:35-40, ESV, EMPHASIS ADDED

*"...And he said to them, "If anyone would be first, he must be last of all **and** servant of all."*

— MARK 9:35, ESV, EMPHASIS ADDED

*"When he had washed their feet and put on his outer garments and resumed his place, he said to them, "Do you understand what I have done to you? You call me Teacher and Lord, and you are right, for so I am. If I then, your Lord and Teacher, have washed your feet, you also ought to wash one another's feet. For I have given you an example, that you also should do just as I have done to you. Truly, truly, I say to you, a servant is not greater than his master, nor is a messenger greater than the one who sent him. (**And**) If you know these things, blessed are you if you do them."*

— JOHN 13:12-17, ESV, ADDITION MINE

AND

I know there is nothing in me
that can drum up love;
nothing in me that can love like You,
willing to sacrifice everything comfortable.
There's nothing in me that can
look past the erected barbed barriers of self-protec-
tion or pain in others
("though perhaps for a good man one will choose to
die...")
Except You...

Living Bread from heaven
Spirit of the Living God
Father Creator Lover of all
Fallen on, Within me,

Living, breathing,
BEING;
Inviting to Love.
Wherever I am.
I want to go higher,
'nearer my God to Thee,'
beyond the horizons of what I know,
have lived to date;
conceive in me
Your new, even now.

How far will You s t r e t c h me?
What MORE will You bring to birth?

— PART X —

THE LAST WORD

*"And He [further] said to me,
It is done!
I am the Alpha and the Omega,
the Beginning and the End.
To the thirsty I [Myself] will give water
without price
from the fountain (springs)
of the water of Life."*

Revelation 21:6, AMPC

53

LAST WORD

Feeling so conscious that for all the words in all the languages in the world, none are so lovely, so not needing of definition, so peaceful and powerful, as Jesus. He is the One High and Lifted Up, the One worthy of all praise, the only One Who is pure, Who is true, Who is needed. We do not need any other word to describe the Word of God Himself, this One Who came to show us what His desiring-close-relationship Father was like, though we have filled many books trying.

If we will truly listen, hearing with the ears of our heart, we will discover that all we ever need to hear, to speak, is Jesus.

"You Are Beautiful Beyond Description," Mark Altrogge's song,[1] speaks of the beauty and wonder of God that inspires complete awe. Its beautiful chorus states simply, "I stand in awe of You." What powerful words, and how very true. In a sense, Jesus is the Last Word—He is all in all.

Last Word[2] (noun)

- The final word or speech, regarded as settling the argument, final authority;

- Something regarded as perfect or definitive.

YOU MAKE ME SILLY

Glorious Ancient of Days
Who is my Papa;
Bright Morning Star
Who is my Friend;
Spirit of God
Who is my Counsellor,
I stand
and bow
and play
and live

in awe of You!

You Who ARE the great
I AM,
I marvel at You Who ARE:
my Friend!
Too marv'lous for words,
You word my heart

that I may sing
and dance,
impart

Yours!

Seen of the unseen,
exact representation;
You Who IS Word, named
Faithful, True,
rode Your white stallion
brought Your battalion
right into my heart to
let me see You.

Though awe renders speechless
You've not left me voiceless,
but given a paintbrush
conveying Your face;
movingly tender,
eyes Fire lit with Life,
incredibly kind
removing all strife
of rigid destruction;
intensely near,
demolishing fear,
held,

always,

right here,

Under Your wing.

My sweet succourer
as nectar to
extincting bees,
You brought me back from death's dark edge,
deep well of tears
long gone, my Friend:

Awe,

and then You tickle me and we go laughing, running,
    shrieking in Joy among those nectar-full, bee-
    nosed in flowers.

King of Heaven, You are Mine.
Lord of all lords, I am Thine,
You make me silly,
all willy-nilly,
offensively frilly
to all who love rules...
no longer bound there,
now (mostly) found where
freedom abounds in Your
Garden.

Ha!

Who knew Peas could fly!

"I saw in the night visions, and behold, on the clouds of the heavens came One like a Son of man, and He came to the Ancient of Days and was presented before Him. And there was given Him [the Messiah] dominion and glory and kingdom, that all peoples, nations, and languages should serve Him. His dominion is an everlasting dominion which shall not pass away, and His kingdom is one which shall not be destroyed."

— DANIEL 7:13-14, AMPC (WRITTEN IN
605-530 BC)

"Then I turned to see [whose was] the voice that was speaking to me, and on turning I saw seven golden lampstands, And in the midst of the lampstands [One] like a Son of Man, clothed with a robe which reached to His feet and with a girdle of gold about His breast. His head and His hair were white like white wool, [as white] as snow, and His eyes [flashed] like a flame of fire. His feet glowed like burnished (bright) bronze as it is refined in a furnace, and His voice was like the sound of many waters. In His right hand He held seven stars, and from His mouth there came forth a sharp two-edged sword, and His face was like the sun shining in full power at midday. When I saw Him, I fell at His feet as if dead. But He laid His right hand on me and said, Do not be afraid! I am the First and the Last, And the Ever-living One [I am living in the eternity of the eternities]. I died, but see, I am alive forevermore; and I possess the keys of death and Hades (the realm of the dead)."

— REVELATION 1:12-18, AMPC (WRITTEN
APPROXIMATELY 70 AD)

"I am the Root (the Source) and the Offspring of David, the radiant and brilliant Morning Star. The [Holy] Spirit and the bride... say, Come! And let him who is listening say, Come! And let everyone come who is thirsty [who is painfully conscious of his need of those things by which the soul is refreshed, supported, and strengthened]; and whoever [earnestly] desires to do it, let him come, take, appropriate, and drink the water of Life without cost."

— REVELATION 22:16B-17, AMPC

Activations For Learning to Be Loved

LAST WORD

Breath of Life ~

"Here I AM
Be Loved!
Live knowing you are Loved, ALWAYS!"

Selah ~

Here you are, before the Lamb Lion of God, the One Who has pursued you, offering His hand, His shelter, His strength, His life. The Victorious Brilliant Shining One, Lord of ALL... yet your Friend. What aspect of awe comes as you stand, bow, kneel silently before Jesus?

On That Note ~

What a Beautiful Name by Hillsong Worship; *Last Word* by Elevation Worship; *I Am the Day* by Libera; and *Sanctus* by Fernando Ortega

Pray the Word ~

Amen. Come Lord Jesus!

EPILOGUE

*I*t gives me great pleasure to tell you that Pip has grown by leaps and bounds in being comfortable with love. She revels in contact, even allowing me to hold her purring self – it only took nine years of continuing tenderness and care, building trust and relationship together. My heart swells with thanksgiving and love for her, enjoying her unique personality.

Continuing our recognition of how Pip's and my relationship is a parallel to our Abba's interaction with us kids, we can marvel at His patient caring in our lives. How joyful He must be as we become more comfortable, even hungry, to come rest in His love, fully trusting Him!

A couple of months following the writing of *Learning to Be Loved* but before the publishing process was able to begin, an event took place that tested every word and promise shared in this book.

My husband Grant and I had much opportunity to step into and believe how deeply we are beloved, held, and safe in our

Father's heart and arms. Grant had a sudden stroke in January 2019, followed by many bouts of aspiration pneumonia. It quickly became very serious, and he was not expected to live. Grant ended up spending six weeks in the ICU, over three months in the hospital in total, being released to come home to my traumatised care on April 27th, 2019.

Our journey through the days and months that followed, how Jesus met with us (and how He didn't), how Holy Spirit comforted, how our Abba held us, affirming His promises of Presence, of our beloved-ness in Him, is what has birthed the sequel to *Learning to Be Loved*.

Living Loved will (in part) chronicle the journey of being led and carried through unimaginable shock and trauma, sharing how our God comforted, cared for, and met us in many different ways. It will retell the sharing of His whispers, His silence, and His encouragements to keep going—one day, one step, one second at a time—as we were called to trust in the midst of great unknowing.

How about you? What has your last year been like? Have you barely held on by the skin of your teeth? Have you known you've been held while in the eye of a storm? Have you laughed in the face of seeming disaster? Have you crumpled in tears over and over? Have you danced as a child, loved? Has each millisecond presented an opportunity to choose trust?

Some of Abba's first words, which I journaled when I finally had time to sit quiet and listen, three days after Grant's stroke, were these:

"I AM here; I AM with you.
Have no fear for anything – I will not take him from you
– rather, the opposite – this is the time for miracles!"

The Last Word, the
One Whose hand continues held out before you,
Whose Name is above all Names,
Whose eyes are tenderly upon you,
Whose heart is with, within you,
Whose Power and Kindness has never left you,

the Last Word,
in all His Glorious full of Authority Magnificence,

still and always,

is

Jesus."

APPENDIX
HOW TO HEAR GOD'S VOICE

By Mark Virkler,
used by permission

She had done it again! Instead of coming straight home from school like she was supposed to, she had gone to her friend's house. Without permission. Without our knowledge. Without doing her chores.

With a ministering household that included remnants of three struggling families plus our own toddler and newborn, my wife simply couldn't handle all the work on her own. Everyone had to pull their own weight. Everyone had age-appropriate tasks they were expected to complete. At fourteen, Rachel and her younger brother were living with us while her parents tried to overcome lifestyle patterns that had resulted in the children running away to escape the dysfunction. I felt sorry for Rachel, but, honestly my wife was my greatest concern.

Now Rachel had ditched her chores to spend time with her friends. It wasn't the first time, but if I had anything to say about it, it would be the last. I intended to lay down the law when she got home and make it very clear that if she was going to live under my roof, she would obey my rules.

But...she wasn't home yet. And I had recently been learning to hear God's voice more clearly. Maybe I should try to see if I could hear anything from Him about the situation. Maybe He could give me a way to get her to do what she was supposed to (i.e. what I wanted her to do). So I went to my office and reviewed what the Lord had been teaching me from Habakkuk 2:1,2: "I will stand on my guard post and station myself on the rampart; And I will keep watch to see what He will speak to me...Then the Lord answered me and said, 'Record the vision....'"

Habakkuk said, "I will stand on my guard post..." (Hab. 2:1). The first key to hearing God's voice is to go to a quiet place and still our own thoughts and emotions. Psalm 46:10 encourages us to be still, let go, cease striving, and know that He is God. In Psalm 37:7 we are called to "be still before the Lord and wait patiently for Him." There is a deep inner knowing in our spirits that each of us can experience when we quiet our flesh and our minds. Practicing the art of biblical meditation helps silence the outer noise and distractions clamoring for our attention.

I didn't have a guard post but I did have an office, so I went there to quiet my temper and my mind. Loving God through a quiet worship song is one very effective way to become still. In 2 Kings 3, Elisha needed a word from the Lord so he said, "Bring me a minstrel," and as the minstrel played, the Lord spoke. I have found that playing a worship song on my autoharp is the quickest way for me to come to stillness. I need to choose my song carefully; boisterous songs of praise do not bring me to stillness, but rather gentle songs that express my love and worship. And it isn't enough just to sing the song into the cosmos – I come into the Lord's presence most quickly and easily when I use my godly imagination to see the truth that He is right here with me and I sing my songs to Him, personally.

"I will keep watch to see," said the prophet. To receive the pure word of God, it is very important that my heart be properly focused as I become still, because my focus is the source of the intuitive flow. If I fix my eyes upon Jesus (Heb. 12:2), the intuitive flow comes from Jesus. But if I fix my gaze upon some desire of my heart, the intuitive flow comes out of that desire. To have a pure flow I must become still and carefully fix my eyes upon Jesus. Quietly worshiping the King and receiving out of the stillness that follows quite easily accomplishes this.

So I used the second key to hearing God's voice: As you pray, fix the eyes of your heart upon Jesus, seeing in the Spirit the dreams and visions of Almighty God. Habakkuk was actually looking for vision as he prayed. He opened the eyes of his heart, and looked into the spirit world to see what God wanted to show him.

God has always spoken through dreams and visions, and He specifically said that they would come to those upon whom the Holy Spirit is poured out (Acts 2:1-4, 17).

Being a logical, rational person, observable facts that could be verified by my physical senses were the foundations of my life, including my spiritual life. I had never thought of opening the eyes of my heart and looking for vision. However, I have come to believe that this is exactly what God wants me to do. He gave me eyes in my heart to see in the spirit the vision and movement of Almighty God. There is an active spirit world all around us, full of angels, demons, the Holy Spirit, the omnipresent Father, and His omnipresent Son, Jesus. The only reasons for me not to see this reality are unbelief or lack of knowledge.

In his sermon in Acts 2:25, Peter refers to King David's statement: "I saw the Lord always in my presence; for He is at my right hand, so that I will not be shaken." The original psalm makes it clear that this was a decision of David's, not a constant supernatural visitation: "I have set (literally, I have placed) the Lord continually before me; because He is at my right hand, I will not be shaken" (Ps.16:8). Because David knew that the Lord was always with him, he determined in his spirit to see that truth with the eyes of his heart as he went through life, knowing that this would keep his faith strong.

In order to see, we must look. Daniel saw a vision in his mind and said, "I was looking...I kept looking...I kept looking" (Dan. 7:2, 9, 13). As I pray, I look for Jesus, and I watch as He speaks to me, doing and saying the things that are on His heart. Many Christians will find that if they will only look, they will see. Jesus is Emmanuel, God with us (Matt. 1:23). It is as simple as that. You can see Christ present with you because Christ is present with you. In fact, the vision may come so easily that you will be tempted to reject it, thinking that it is just you. But if you persist in recording these visions, your doubt will soon be overcome by faith as you recognize that the content of them could only be birthed in Almighty God.

Jesus demonstrated the ability of living out of constant contact with God, declaring that He did nothing on His own initiative, but only what He saw the Father doing, and heard the Father saying (Jn. 5:19,20,30). What an incredible way to live!

Is it possible for us to live out of divine initiative as Jesus did? Yes! We must simply fix our eyes upon Jesus. The veil has been torn, giving access into the immediate presence of God, and He calls us to draw near (Lk. 23:45; Heb. 10:19-22). "I pray that the eyes of your heart will be enlightened...."

When I had quieted my heart enough that I was able to picture Jesus without the distractions of my own ideas and plans, I was able to "keep watch to see what He will speak to me." I wrote down my question: "Lord, what should I do about Rachel?"

Immediately the thought came to me, "She is insecure." Well, that certainly wasn't my thought! Her behavior looked like rebellion to me, not insecurity.

But like Habakkuk, I was coming to know the sound of God speaking to me (Hab. 2:2). Elijah described it as a still, small voice (I Kings 19:12). I had previously listened for an inner audible voice, and God does speak that way at times. However, I have found that usually, God's voice comes as spontaneous thoughts, visions, feelings, or impressions.

For example, haven't you been driving down the road and had a thought come to you to pray for a certain person? Didn't you believe it was God telling you to pray? What did God's voice sound like? Was it an audible voice, or was it a spontaneous thought that lit upon your mind?

Experience indicates that we perceive spirit-level communication as spontaneous thoughts, impressions and visions, and Scripture confirms this in many ways. For example, one definition of paga, a Hebrew word for intercession, is "a chance encounter or an accidental intersecting." When God lays people on our hearts, He does it through paga, a chance-encounter thought "accidentally" intersecting our minds.

So the third key to hearing God's voice is recognizing that God's voice in your heart often sounds like a flow of spontaneous thoughts. Therefore, when I want to hear from God, I tune to chance-encounter or spontaneous thoughts.

Finally, God told Habakkuk to record the vision (Hab. 2:2). This was not an isolated command. The Scriptures record many examples of individual's prayers and God's replies, such as the Psalms, many of the prophets, and Revelation. I have found that obeying this final principle amplified my confidence in my ability to hear God's voice so that I could finally make living out of His initiatives a way of life. The fourth key, two-way journaling or the writing out of your prayers and God's answers, brings great freedom in hearing God's voice.

I have found two-way journaling to be a fabulous catalyst for clearly discerning God's inner, spontaneous flow, because as I journal I am able to write in faith for long periods of time, simply believing it is God. I know that what I believe I have received from God must be tested. However, testing involves doubt and doubt blocks divine communication, so I do not want to test while I am trying to receive. (See James 1:5-8.) With journaling, I can receive in faith, knowing that when the flow has ended I can test and examine it carefully.

So I wrote down what I believed He had said: "She is insecure."

But the Lord wasn't done. I continued to write the spontaneous thoughts that came to me: "Love her unconditionally. She is flesh of your flesh and bone of your bone."

My mind immediately objected: She is not flesh of my flesh. She is not related to me at all – she is a foster child, just living in my home temporarily. It was definitely time to test this "word from the Lord"!

There are three possible sources of thoughts in our minds: ourselves, satan and the Holy Spirit. It was obvious that the words in my journal did not come from my own mind – I certainly didn't see her as insecure or flesh of my flesh. And I sincerely doubted that satan would encourage me to love anyone unconditionally!

Okay, it was starting to look like I might have actually received counsel from the Lord. It was consistent with the names and character of God as revealed in the Scripture, and totally contrary to the names and character of the enemy. So that meant that I was hearing from the Lord, and He wanted me to see the situation in a different light. Rachel was my daughter – part of my family not by blood but by the hand of God Himself. The chaos of her birth home had created deep insecurity about her worthiness to be loved by anyone, including me and including God. Only the unconditional love of the Lord expressed through an imperfect human would reach her heart.

But there was still one more test I needed to perform before I would have absolute confidence that this was truly God's word to me: I needed confirmation from someone else whose spiritual discernment I trusted. So I went to my wife and shared what I had received. I knew if I could get her validation, especially since she was the one most wronged in the situation, then I could say, at least to myself, "Thus sayeth the Lord."

Needless to say, Patti immediately and without question confirmed that the Lord had spoken to me. My entire planned lecture was forgotten. I returned to my office anxious to hear more. As the Lord planted a new, supernatural love for Rachel within me, He showed me what to say and how to say it to not only address the current issue of household responsibility, but the deeper issues of love and acceptance and worthiness.

Rachel and her brother remained as part of our family for another two years, giving us many opportunities to demonstrate and teach about the Father's love, planting spiritual seeds in thirsty soil. We weren't perfect and we didn't solve all of her issues, but because I had learned to listen to the Lord, we were able to avoid creating more brokenness and separation.

The four simple keys that the Lord showed me from Habakkuk have been used by people of all ages, from four to a hundred and four, from every continent, culture and denomination, to break through into intimate two-way conversations with their loving Father and dearest Friend. Omitting any one of the keys will prevent you from receiving all He wants to say to you. The order of the keys is not important, just that you use them all. Embracing all four, by faith, can change your life. Simply quiet yourself down, tune to spontaneity, look for vision, and journal. He is waiting to meet you there.

You will be amazed when you journal! Doubt may hinder you at first, but throw it off, reminding yourself that it is a biblical concept, and that God is present, speaking to His children. Relax. When we cease our labors and enter His rest, God is free to flow (Heb. 4:10).

Why not try it for yourself, right now? Sit back comfortably, take out your pen and paper, and smile. Turn your attention toward the Lord in praise and worship, seeking His face. Many people have found the music and visionary prayer called "A Stroll Along the Sea of Galilee" helpful in getting them started. You can listen to it and download it free at www.CWGMinistries.org/Galilee.

After you write your question to Him, become still, fixing your gaze on Jesus. You will suddenly have a very good thought. Don't doubt it; simply write it down. Later, as you read your journaling, you, too, will be blessed to discover that you are indeed dialoguing with God. If you wonder if it is really the Lord speaking to you, share it with your spouse or a friend. Their input will encourage your faith and strengthen your commitment to spend time getting to know the Lover of your soul more intimately than you ever dreamed possible.

Is It Really God?

Five ways to be sure what you're hearing is from Him:

1)   Test the Origin (1 Jn. 4:1)

Thoughts from our own minds are progressive, with one thought leading to the next, however tangentially. Thoughts from the spirit world are spontaneous. The Hebrew word for true prophecy is naba, which literally means to bubble up, whereas false prophecy is ziyd meaning to boil up. True words from the Lord will bubble up from our innermost being; we don't need to cook them up ourselves.

2)   Compare It to Biblical Principles

God will never say something to you personally which is contrary to His universal revelation as expressed in the Scriptures. If the Bible clearly states that something is a sin, no amount of journaling can make it right. Much of what you journal about will not be specifically addressed in the Bible, however, so an understanding of biblical principles is also needed.

3) Compare It to the Names and Character of God as Revealed in the Bible

Anything God says to you will be in harmony with His essential nature. Journaling will help you get to know God personally, but knowing what the Bible says about Him will help you discern what words are from Him. Make sure the tenor of your journaling lines up with the character of God as described in the names of the Father, Son and Holy Spirit.

4)   Test the Fruit (Matt. 7:15-20)

What effect does what you are hearing have on your soul and your spirit? Words from the Lord will quicken your faith and increase your love, peace and joy. They will stimulate a sense of humility within you as you become more aware of Who God is and who you are. On the other hand, any words you receive which cause you to fear or doubt, which bring you into confusion or anxiety, or which stroke your ego (especially if you hear something that is "just for you alone – no one else is worthy") must be immediately rebuked and rejected as lies of the enemy.

5) Share It with Your Spiritual Counselors (Prov. 11:14)

We are members of a Body! A cord of three strands is not easily broken and God's intention has always been for us to grow together. Nothing will increase your faith in your ability to hear from God like having it confirmed by two or three other people! Share it with your spouse, your parents, your friends, your elder, your group leader, even your grown children can be your sounding board. They don't need to be perfect or super-spiritual; they just need to love you, be committed to being available to you, have a solid biblical orientation, and most importantly, they must also willingly and easily receive counsel. Avoid the authoritarian who insists that because of their standing in the church or with God, they no longer need to listen to others. Find two or three people and let them confirm that you are hearing from God!

The book *4 Keys to Hearing God's Voice* is available at www.CWGMinistries.org.

NOTES

Dedication

1. "Bible Gateway Footnote b: Matthew 9:12 - New English Translation." Bible Gateway. Biblical Studies Press, LLC. Accessed September 9, 2020. https://www.biblegateway.com/passage/?search=matthew 9:12.

Introduction

1. Soroski, Jason. "What Does Selah Mean in the Bible and Why Is It Important?" Crosswalk.com. Salem Web Network, October 10, 2018. https://www.crosswalk.com/faith/bible-study/what-does-selah-mean.html.
2. Noyes, Penny. "What Does Selah Mean in the Bible?" Christianity.com. Salem Web Network, April 24, 2019. https://www.christianity.com/wiki/christian-terms/what-does-selah-mean-in-the-bible.html.
3. See Psalm 40:3.
4. Nouwen, Henri, *Life of the Beloved*, p.39, 1992, New York, NY, Crossword Publishing Co.
5. Communion With God Ministries at https://www.cwgministries.org/.

1. The Living Word

1. "The Word became flesh and blood, and moved into the neighborhood. We saw the glory with our own eyes, the one-of-a-kind glory, like Father, like Son, Generous inside and out, true from start to finish." – John 1:14 (MSG)
2. "For the Word that God speaks is alive and full of power [making it active, operative, energizing, and effective]; it is sharper than any two-edged sword, penetrating to the dividing line of the breath of life (soul) and [the immortal] spirit, and of joints and marrow [of the deepest parts of our nature], exposing and sifting and analyzing and judging the very thoughts and purposes of the heart." – Hebrews 4:12 (AMPC)

2. Sabbatical

1. "Sabbatical." Dictionary.com. Dictionary.com. Accessed September 9, 2020. https://www.dictionary.com/browse/sabbatical?s=t.
2. "Sabbatical Year." Dictionary.com. Dictionary.com. Accessed September 9, 2020. https://www.dictionary.com/browse/sabbatical-year?s=t.
3. See Exodus 25:8-11 and Leviticus 25.
4. Vallotton, Kris. *Spirit Wars: Winning the Invisible Battle against Sin and the Enemy* (Kindle Edition). Bloomington, MN: Chosen Books, 2012.
5. See Matthew 11:28-30 (MSG).

3. Rest, Restore, and Refresh

1. "Rest." Dictionary.com. Accessed September 9, 2020. https://www.dictionary.com/browse/rest?s=t.
2. "Restore." Cambridge English Dictionary. Accessed September 10, 2020. https://dictionary.cambridge.org/us/dictionary/english/restore.
3. "Refresh." The Free Dictionary. Farlex. Accessed September 9, 2020. https://www.thefreedictionary.com/refresh.
4. "Rest." Dictionary.com. Accessed September 9, 2020. https://www.dictionary.com/browse/rest?s=t.
5. "Restore." Cambridge English Dictionary. Accessed September 10, 2020. https://dictionary.cambridge.org/us/dictionary/english/restore.
6. "Refresh." The Free Dictionary. Farlex. Accessed September 9, 2020. https://www.thefreedictionary.com/refresh.
7. "Restore." Cambridge English Dictionary. Accessed September 10, 2020. https://dictionary.cambridge.org/us/dictionary/english/restore.
8. See Luke 9:23, New King James Version (NKJV).

4. Choice

1. "Choice." Dictionary.com. Accessed September 9, 2020. https://www.dictionary.com/browse/choice?s=t.
2. Cameron, Julia. "July 17." Essay. In *The Artist's Way Every Day: A Year of Creative Living*. New York: Jeremy P. Tarcher/Penguin, 2009.

5. Soaking

1. "Soaking," dictionary.com, accessed July 15, 2020, https://www.dictionary.com/browse/soaking?s=t.
2. From Luke 12:22-32

6. Breathe ~ Resuscitate

1. "The Oxygen Machine - Science NetLinks." n.d. Sciencenetlinks.Com. Accessed July 28, 2020. http://www.sciencenetlinks.com/lessons/oxygen-machine/.
2. "Breath." Dictionary.com, accessed July 28, 2020. https://www.dictionary.com/browse/breath?s=t.
3. "Resuscitate." Oxford Dictionary on Lexico.com, accessed July 28, 2020. https://www.lexico.com/definition/resuscitate.
4. "What Is Another Word for Resuscitate? Resuscitate Synonyms - Word-Hippo Thesaurus." WordHippo, 2020. https://www.wordhippo.com/what-is/another-word-for/resuscitate.html.

7. Cease Striving

1. "Striving." Dictionary.com, accessed July 28, 2020. https://www.dictionary.com/browse/striving?s=t.
2. "Striving." Collins Dictionary, accessed July 28, 2020. https://www.collinsdictionary.com/dictionary/english/striving.
3. See Isaiah 30:15, NIV.

8. Replenish

1. "Replenish." Dictionary.com, accessed July 28, 2020. https://www.dictionary.com/browse/replenish?s=t.

9. Love

1. "Love." Oxford Dictionary on Lexico.com, accessed July 19, 2020. https://www.lexico.com/definition/love.
2. See Ephesians 3:18-19.
3. See 1 Corinthians 2:9-10.
4. See Ephesians 3:20.
5. See Psalm 139:13-18 and Jeremiah 1:5.

10. Coming Home

1. "Prodigal." Dictionary.com, accessed July 19, 2020. https://www.dictionary.com/browse/prodigal?s=t.

11. Safety

1. "Safety." Dictionary.com, accessed July 19, 2020. https://www.dictionary.com/browse/safety?s=t.
2. See Psalm 91:1.
3. See John 14:1-4.

12. Vulnerability

1. "Vulnerability." Oxford Dictionary on Lexico.com, accessed July 20, 2020. https://www.lexico.com/en/definition/vulnerability.

13. Anything For Love

1. "Sacrifice." Dictionary.com, accessed September 13, 2020. https://www.dictionary.com/browse/sacrifice?s=t.

14. Persistence, Part 1

1. "Persistence." Dictionary.com, accessed September 13, 2020. https://www.dictionary.com/browse/persistence?s=t.
2. See Ephesians 2:15; Colossians 2:13-14.

16. Gratitude

1. Publishing, Harvard Health. n.d. "In Praise of Gratitude." Harvard Health. Accessed August 2, 2020. https://health.harvard.edu/mind-and-mood/in-praise-of-gratitude.
2. "142 Gilbert K. Chesterton Quotes." n.d. BrainyQuote. Accessed August 2, 2020. https://www.brainyquote.com/authors/gilbert-k-chesterton-quotes.
3. Cameron, Julia. "December 27." Essay. In *The Artist's Way Every Day: A Year of Creative Living* (New York: Jeremy P. Tarcher/Penguin, 2009), 397.

17. Pentecost

1. See 1 Corinthians 15:4-8.
2. See Acts 1:1-5, 12-14; Acts 2:1-21, 40-43.

18. Compare

1. "Compare." Yourdictionary.com, accessed September 14, 2020. https://www.yourdictionary.com/compare.

19. Listen

1. "Listen." Cambridge Dictionary, accessed September 14, 2020. https://dictionary.cambridge.org/dictionary/english/listen.
2. See John 10:14-15.
3. Virkler, Mark, and Patti Virkler. *4 Keys to Hearing God's Voice* (Shippensburg, PA: Destiny Image Publishers, 2010), 23-24.

20. More

1. From Psalm 131 in the Message Bible, which had spoken very strongly to me on the flight to South Africa.
2. "More." Dictionary.com, accessed September 14, 2020. https://www.dictionary.com/browse/more?s=t.

21. Journey

1. "Journey." Dictionary.com, accessed September 14, 2020. https://www.dictionary.com/browse/journey?s=t.

22. Identity

1. "Carrier." Oxford Dictionary on Lexico.com, accessed September 15, 2020. https://www.lexico.com/definition/carrier.
2. "Casserole." Merriam-Webster accessed September 15, 2020. https://www.merriam-webster.com/dictionary/casserole.
3. "Daughter." Oxford Dictionary on Lexico.com, accessed September 15, 2020. https://www.lexico.com/definition/daughter.
4. See 1 John 3:1.

23. Help

1. "Help," dictionary.com, accessed July 23, 2020, https://www.dictionary.com/browse/help?s=t.

25. Revelation, Loss, and Resurrection

1. "Revelation." Cambridge Dictionary, accessed September 15, 2020. https://dictionary.cambridge.org/dictionary/english/revelation.
2. "Loss." Dictionary.com, accessed September 15, 2020. https://www.dictionary.com/browse/loss?s=t.
3. "Resurrect." Cambridge Dictionary, accessed September 15, 2020. https://dictionary.cambridge.org/dictionary/english/resurrect.

26. Calling

1. "Calling," Merriam-Webster Dictionary, accessed July 24, 2020, https://www.merriam-webster.com/dictionary/calling.
2. "Calling," Collins Dictionary, accessed July 24, 2020, https://www.collinsdictionary.com/dictionary/english/calling.
3. See Psalm 25:10.

27. Freedom From Fear

1. "Entrenched," vocabulary.com, accessed July 24, 2020, https://www.vocabulary.com/dictionary/entrenched.
2. Cherry, Kendra. "How Does Sublimation Influence Your Behavior?" Verywell Mind. Accessed September 16, 2020. https://www.verywellmind.com/what-is-sublimation-in-psychology-4172222.
3. "Fear," Cambridge Dictionary, accessed July 25, 2020, https://dictionary.cambridge.org/us/dictionary/english/fear.

28. Letting Go of Control

1. "Control," Oxford Dictionary, accessed July 25, 2020, https://www.lexico.com/definition/control.
2. For further information, see http://bit.ly/good-therapy-control-issues.

29. Forgiveness

1. "Forgiveness Definition: What Is Forgiveness." Greater Good. Accessed September 17, 2020. https://greatergood.berkeley.edu/topic/forgiveness/definition.
2. "Forgive." Dictionary.com, accessed September 17, 2020. https://www.dictionary.com/browse/forgive?s=t.
3. "Definition for Forgiveness," 2018. AllAboutGod.com, accessed July 25, 2020, https://www.allaboutgod.com/definition-for-forgiveness-faq.htm.
4. See Matthew 18:21-35.
5. See John 5:19 and 14:9.
6. Manning, Brennan. *Abba's Child: the Cry of the Heart for Intimate Belonging* (Colorado Springs: NavPress, 1994), 69.
7. See Isaiah 30:15

30. Sanctuary

1. "Sanctuary." Merriam-Webster.com, accessed September 17, 2020.
2. "Sanctuary." Dictionary.com, accessed September 17, 2020. https://www.dictionary.com/browse/sanctuary?s=t.
3. "Sanctuary." Dictionary.com, accessed September 17, 2020. https://www.dictionary.com/browse/sanctuary?s=t.

31. Liminal Moments

1. Lynn, Warren. "Invitation to Poetry: Going Home." Web log. *Abbey of the Arts* (blog), September 19, 2011. https://abbeyofthearts.com/blog/2011/09/19/invitation-to-poetry-going-home/.
2. "Liminal," Oxford Dictionary by Lexico.com, accessed July 26, 2020, https://www.lexico.com/definition/liminal.
3. Wikipedia Contributors. 2019. "Liminality." Wikipedia. Wikimedia Foundation. April 4, 2019. https://en.wikipedia.org/wiki/Liminality.
4. "Threshold." Yourdictionary.com, accessed September 17, 2020. https://www.yourdictionary.com/threshold.
5. "Threshold." Business Dictionary, accessed September 17, 2020. http://www.businessdictionary.com/definition/threshold.html.
6. "Threshold." Vocabulary.com, accessed September 17, 2020. https://www.vocabulary.com/dictionary/threshold.

32. Melancholy Moments

1. "Melancholy: Synonyms of Melancholy by Oxford Dictionary on Lexico.com Also Antonyms of Melancholy," accessed September 17, 2020. https://www.lexico.com/synonym/melancholy.
2. See Isaiah 42:3 and 43:2.

33. A Dove

1. See John 1:32; Mark 1:10; Matthew 3:16; and Luke 3:22.
2. See Habakkuk 2:3.
3. "Promise." Oxford Dictionary on Lexico.com, accessed September 17, 2020. https://www.lexico.com/definition/promise.

34. It's Time

1. Simmons, Brian. *I Hear His Whisper: 52 Devotions* (Racine, WI: Broad-Street Publishing, 2015), 15.
2. Thank you Susie dN!

35. Joy

1. "Joy," Dictionary.com, accessed September 17, 2020. https://www.dictionary.com/browse/joy?s=t.
2. Other translations use the word *joy* in place of sheer gift.

36. Growing in the Gift

1. See 2 Corinthians 1:20.

37. Expectations

1. "Expectation." Oxford Dictionary on Lexico.com, accessed September 17, 2020. https://www.lexico.com/definition/expectation.
2. Hein, Larry. Quoted in Britton, Bill. "Daily Riches: Expectations Dashed." Richer By Far, October 5, 2014. https://richerbyfar.com/tag/larry-hein/.

38. Rest (again)...and Slaying Giants

1. See Matthew 11:28-30.

39. Slow Down—You Move Too Fast

1. Paul Simon, *The 59th Street Bridge Song (Feelin' Groovy)* (New York: Columbia Records, 1966), https://www.paulsimon.com/song/59th-street-bridge-song-feelin-groovy/.

40. Time

1. See James 4:13-15.
2. "Time." Cambridge Dictionary, accessed September 18, 2020. https://dictionary.cambridge.org/us/dictionary/english/time.
3. "Time." Oxford Dictionary on Lexico.com, accessed September 18, 2020. https://www.lexico.com/definition/time.

41. Dancing Trust

1. "Dance," dictionary.com. Dictionary.com, 2020. https://www.dictionary.com/browse/dance?s=t.
2. Vaibhav, Ankita, July 12, 2018. Answer on the question, "What is full form dance?" *Quora*, accessed September 18, 2020. https://www.quora.com/What-is-full-form-dance.
3. "Trust." Dictionary.com, accessed September 18, 2020. https://www.dictionary.com/browse/trust?s=t.
4. Hannah Whitall Smith. "Quote," Great Thoughts Treasury. Accessed July 27, 2020. http://greatthoughtstreasury.com/index.php/node/463978.
5. Brennan Manning. *Ruthless Trust: A Ragamuffin's Guide to God* (New York: Harper Collins eBooks, 2015), 180, Kindle.

43. Live Loved

1. Manning, Brennan. *Ruthless Trust: The Ragamuffin's Path to God*. New York, NY: HarperCollins, 2000, 147-48.
2. See Matthew 11:28-30 (MSG).
3. See Psalms 27:5, 46:10, 100:4; Isaiah 30:21, 40:31; John 8:36; Galatians 5:1; and 1 John 3:1.

44. Soaring and Stillness

1. "Soar." Dictionary.com, accessed July 27, 2020. https://www.dictionary.com/browse/soar?s=t.
2. *The American Heritage Roget's Thesaurus.* S.v. "stillness." Retrieved July 27, 2020 from https://www.thefreedictionary.com/stillness.
3. See Isaiah 43:19.

45. The Bedrock of Friendship

1. "Bedrock." Dictionary.com. Dictionary.com, 2020. https://www.dictionary.com/browse/bedrock?s=ts.
2. "Friendship." Yourdictionary.com, accessed September 20, 2020. https://www.yourdictionary.com/friend#:~:text=a%20person%20whom%20one%20knows,being%20helpful%2C%20reliable%2C%20etc.
3. "Friendship: Synonyms of Friendship by Oxford Dictionary on Lexico.com Also Antonyms of Friendship," accessed September 20, 2020. https://www.lexico.com/synonym/friendship.
4. "Friendship." Oxford Dictionary on Lexico.com, accessed September 20, 2020. https://www.lexico.com/definition/friendship.

46. Feasting and Fatness!

1. "Starve." Merriam-Webster Dictionary, accessed September 20, 2020. https://www.merriam-webster.com/dictionary/starve.
2. See Genesis 3:1-5.
3. "Fatness Definition and Meaning - Bible Dictionary." biblestudytools.com. Accessed September 21, 2020. https://www.biblestudytools.com/dictionary/fatness/.
4. "Nourish: Definition of Nourish by Oxford Dictionary on Lexico.com Also Meaning of Nourish." Lexico Dictionaries | English. Oxford University Press, 2020. https://www.lexico.com/definition/nourish.
5. See Matthew 16:25.

47. Peace

1. See Philippians 4:7.
2. See Ephesians 2:13-14.
3. "Peace-Shalom (Hebrew Word Study)." Precept Austin, accessed September 21, 2020. https://www.preceptaustin.org/shalom_-_definition.

4. "Peace-Shalom (Greek Word Study)." Precept Austin, accessed September 21, 2020. https://www.preceptaustin.org/peace_eirene.

48. Joy

1. "Joy." Dictionary.com. Dictionary.com, 2020. https://www.dictionary.com/browse/joy?s=t.
2. See Galatians 5:22-23.
3. Cooke, Graham. *From Goodness to Glory* (email to J. Gilbertson), September 5, 2020.
4. See Hebrews 13:8.
5. See Luke 24:13.

50. Entourage

1. See Matthew 25:34-46.
2. See John 1:3 and James 1:17.

52. Higher

1. "Higher - Dictionary Definition." Vocabulary.com, 2020. https://www.vocabulary.com/dictionary/higher.

53. Last Word

1. Mark Altrogge, *I Stand in Awe*. Sovereign Grace Music. https://sovereigngracemusic.org/music/songs/i-stand-in-awe/
2. "Last Word." Last word dictionary definition | last word defined, 2020. https://www.yourdictionary.com/last-word.

ABOUT THE AUTHOR

Janis is an avid reader, loves a good laugh, and has been active in prayer, small group, and music ministries for over 40 years. She loves to recognise and encourage others in their own gifts, and her greatest desire is to let people know they are tenderly loved by God, leading them to be in utter awe of Jesus that their lives may be lived in Restful Joy and Power, fueled by His Spirit.

Janis and her husband Grant live right next door to the beautiful Rocky Mountains in Calgary, Alberta, Canada, where they greatly enjoy spending time with family and building close community with others.